piece of mind

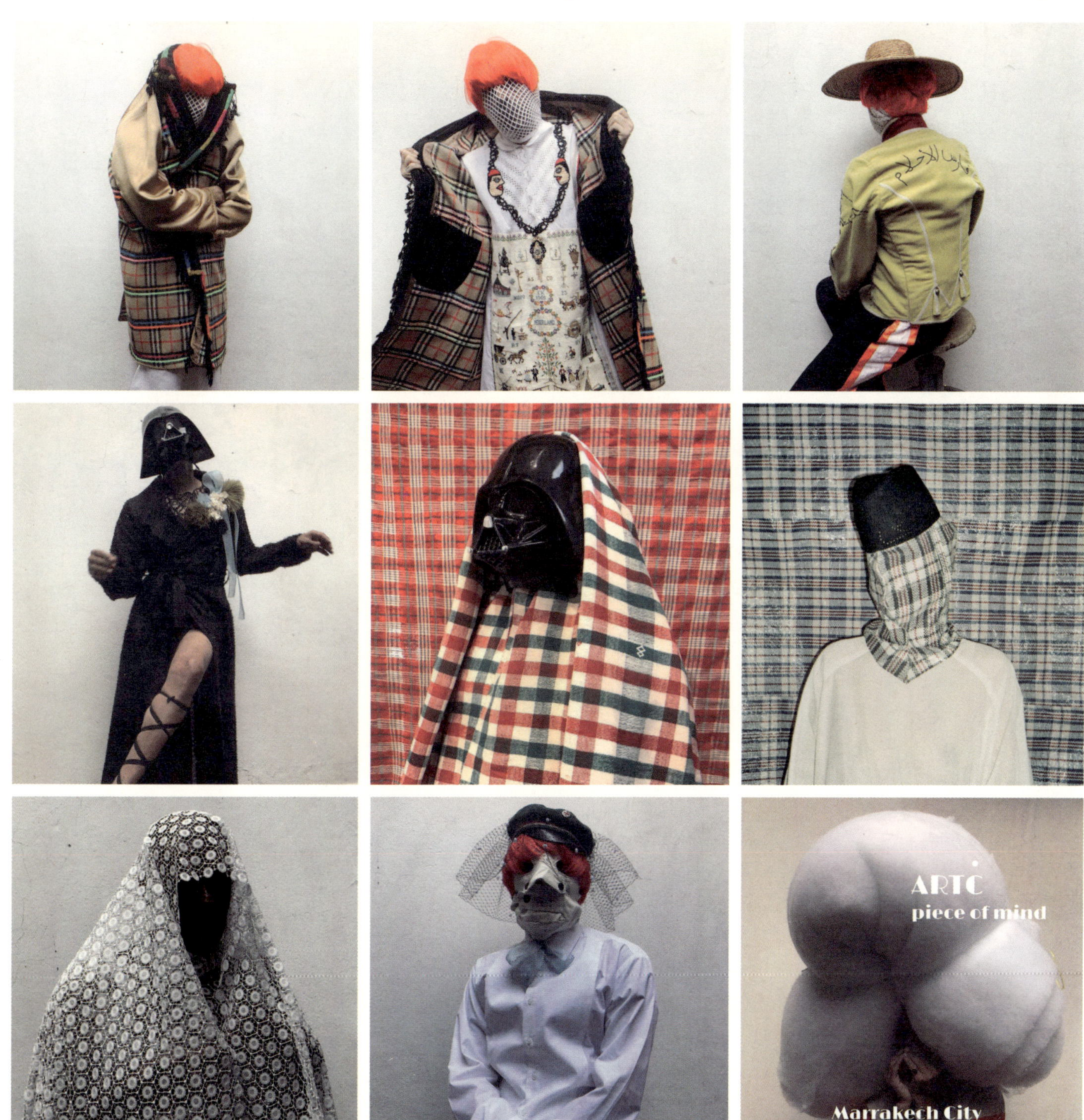
ARTC
piece of mind
Marrakech City

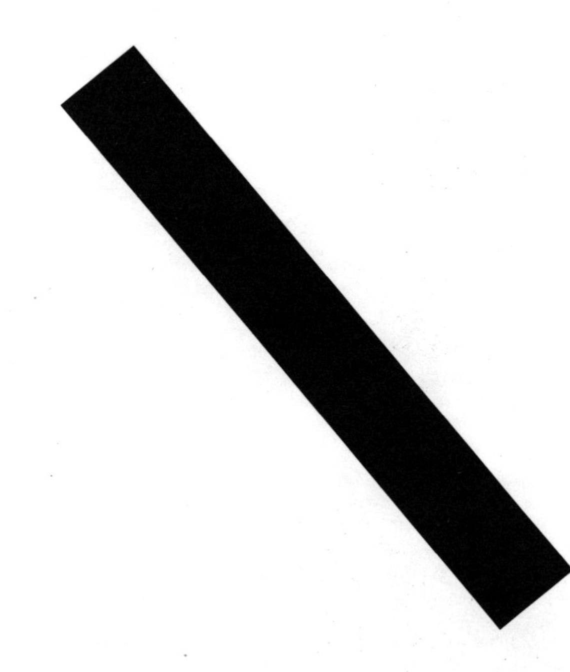

Time that passed is present memories of future hopes. I create all my pieces with a total freedom from the state of mind I have at the moment. Being respectful of the past and the culture to bring something warmer. Vintage fabrics can match past and present. Colors and prints are my landscapes. Napoléon said: **There is a fine line between the ridiculous and the sublime** I search this line every time in every piece. I'm thinking what we would like to have, that we do not have yet. The strongest part we all have is our individuality. That is what I'm doing with one-of-a-kind piece, as we all are.

Artsi Ifrach

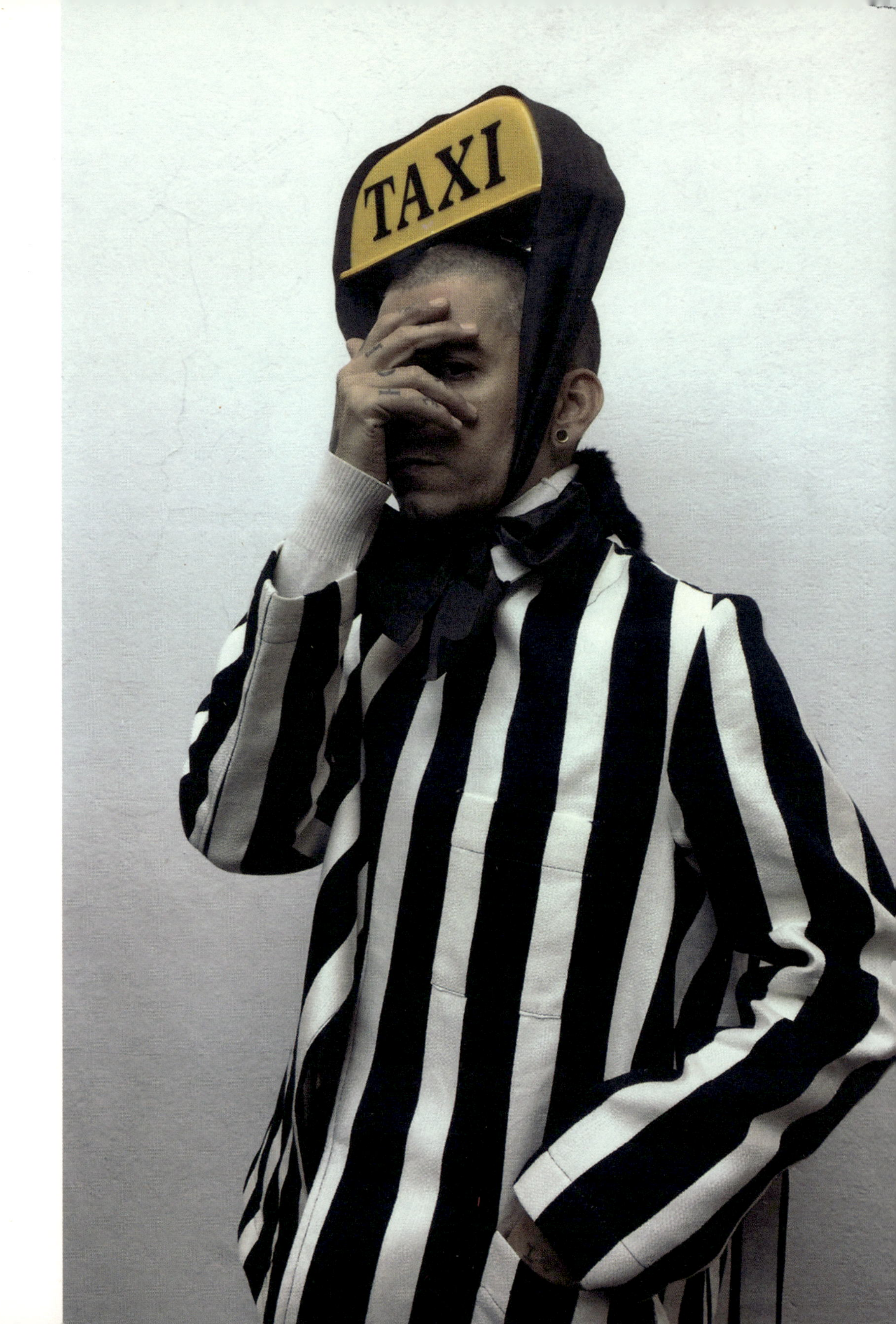
TAXI

ARTĊ
piece of mind

KAHL

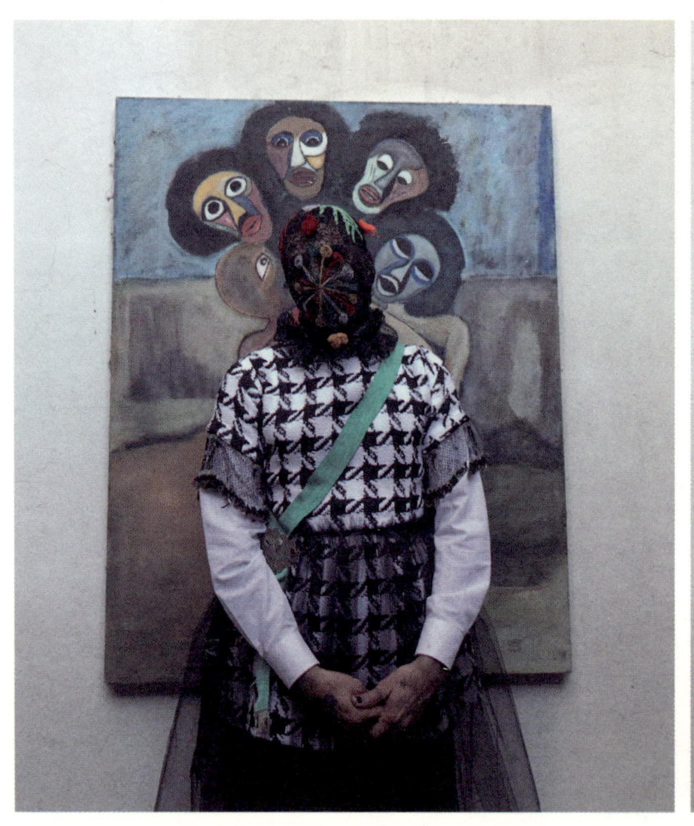

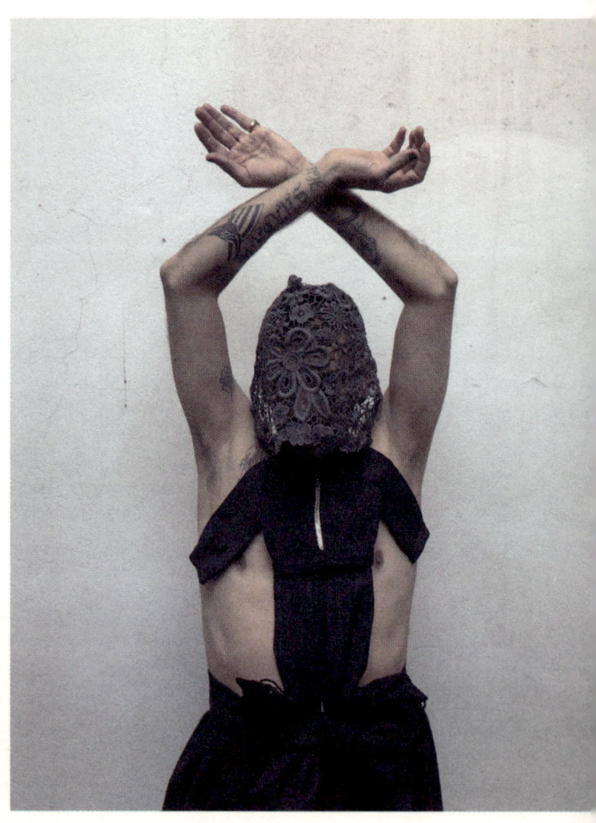

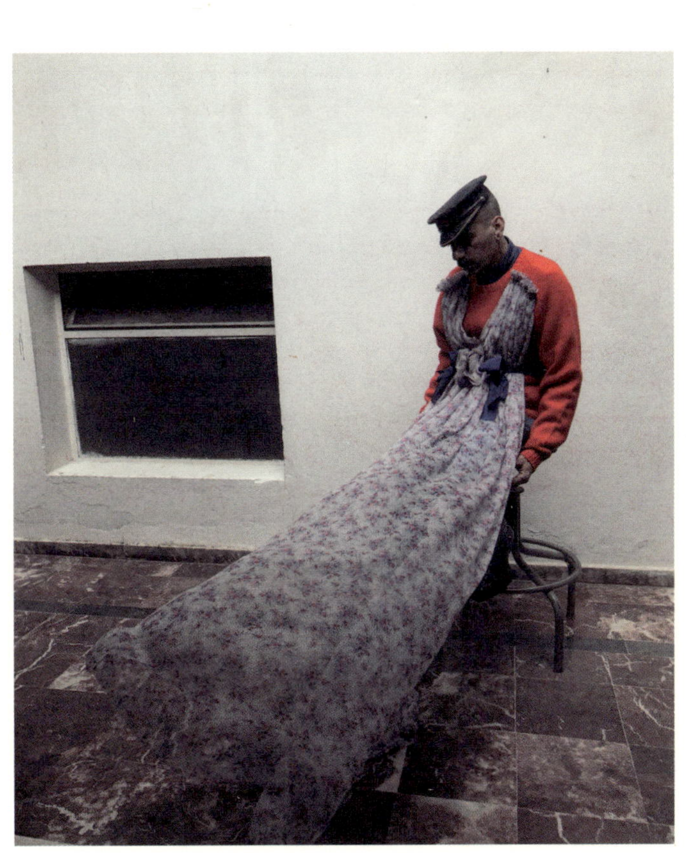

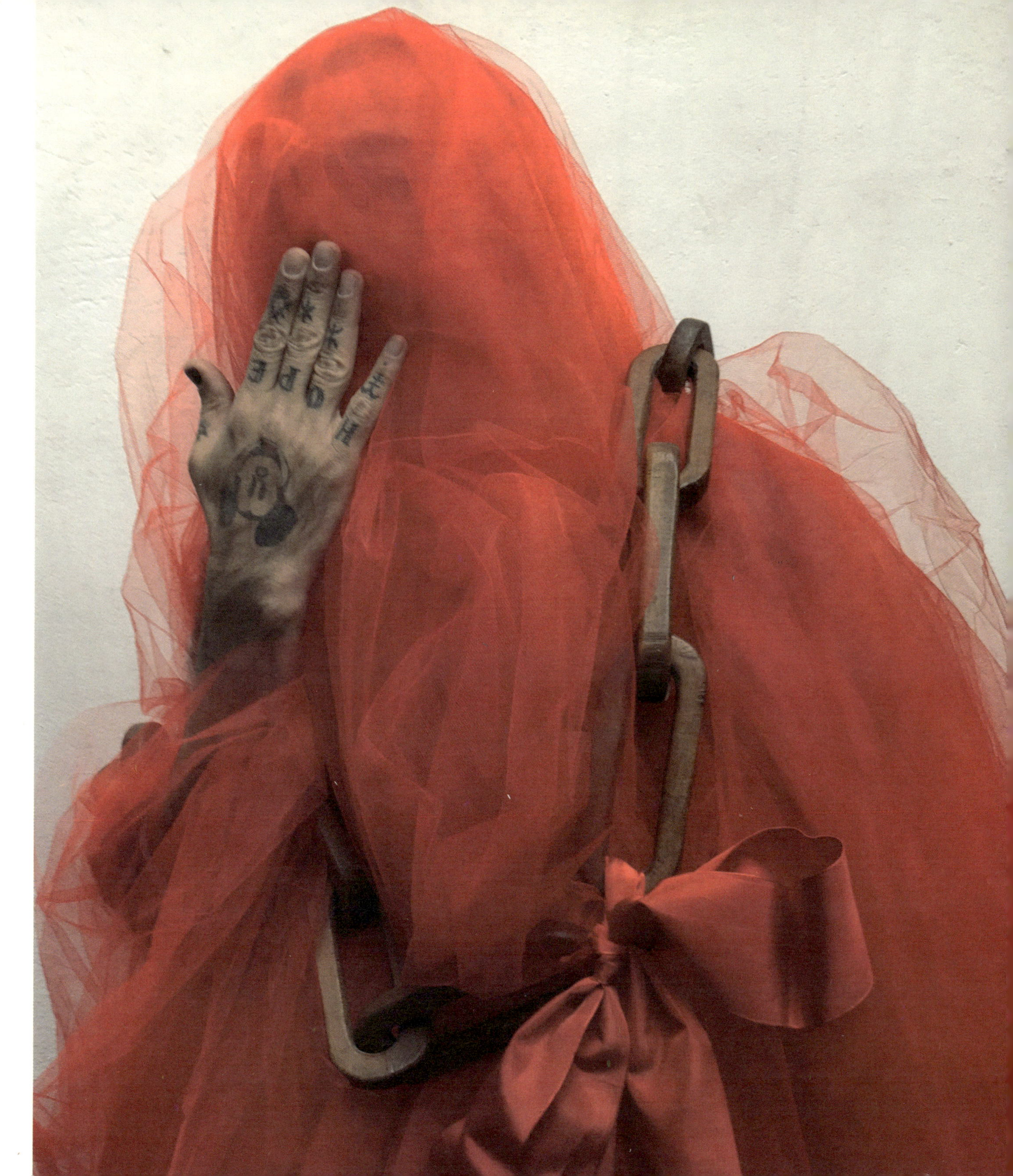

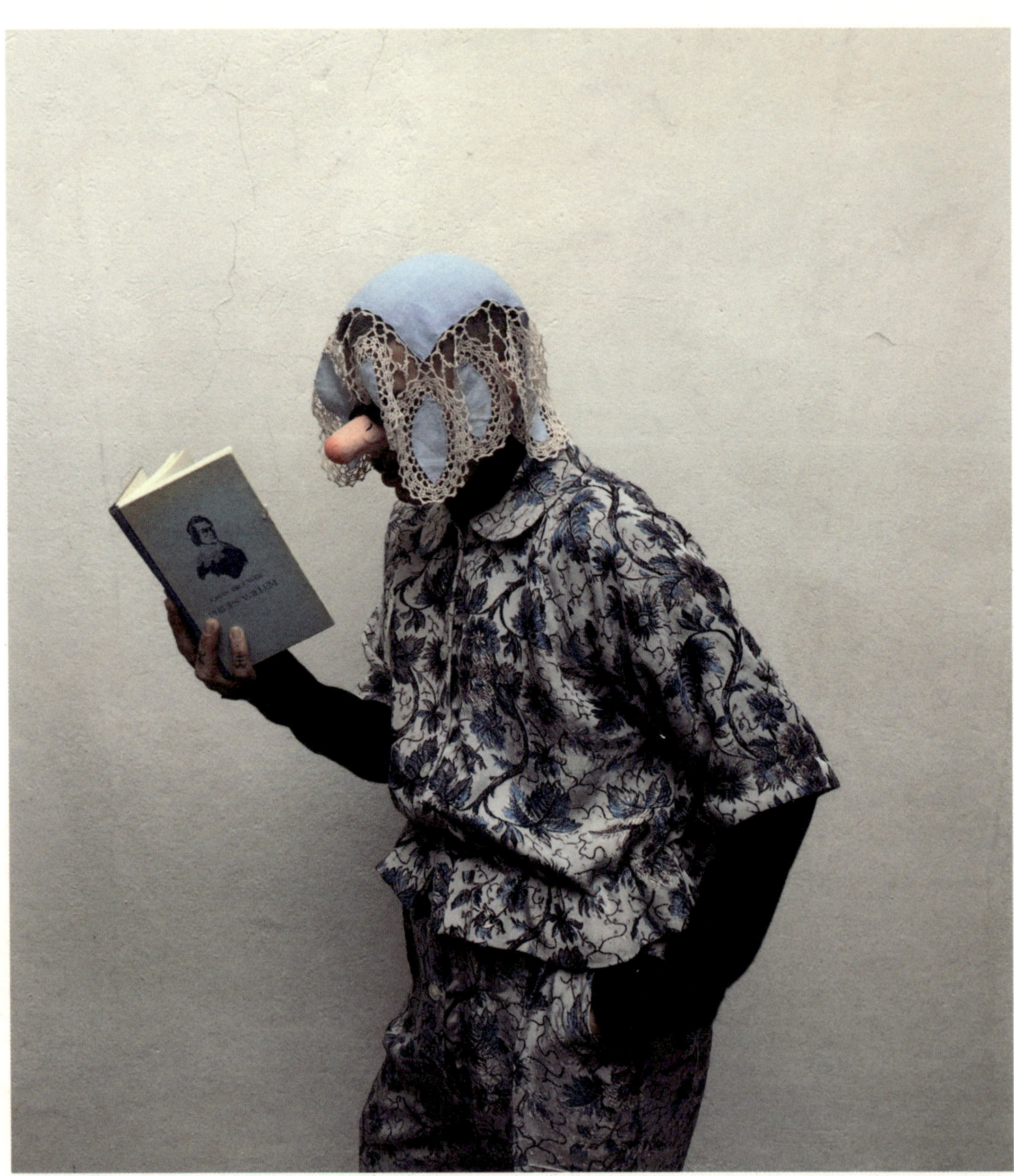

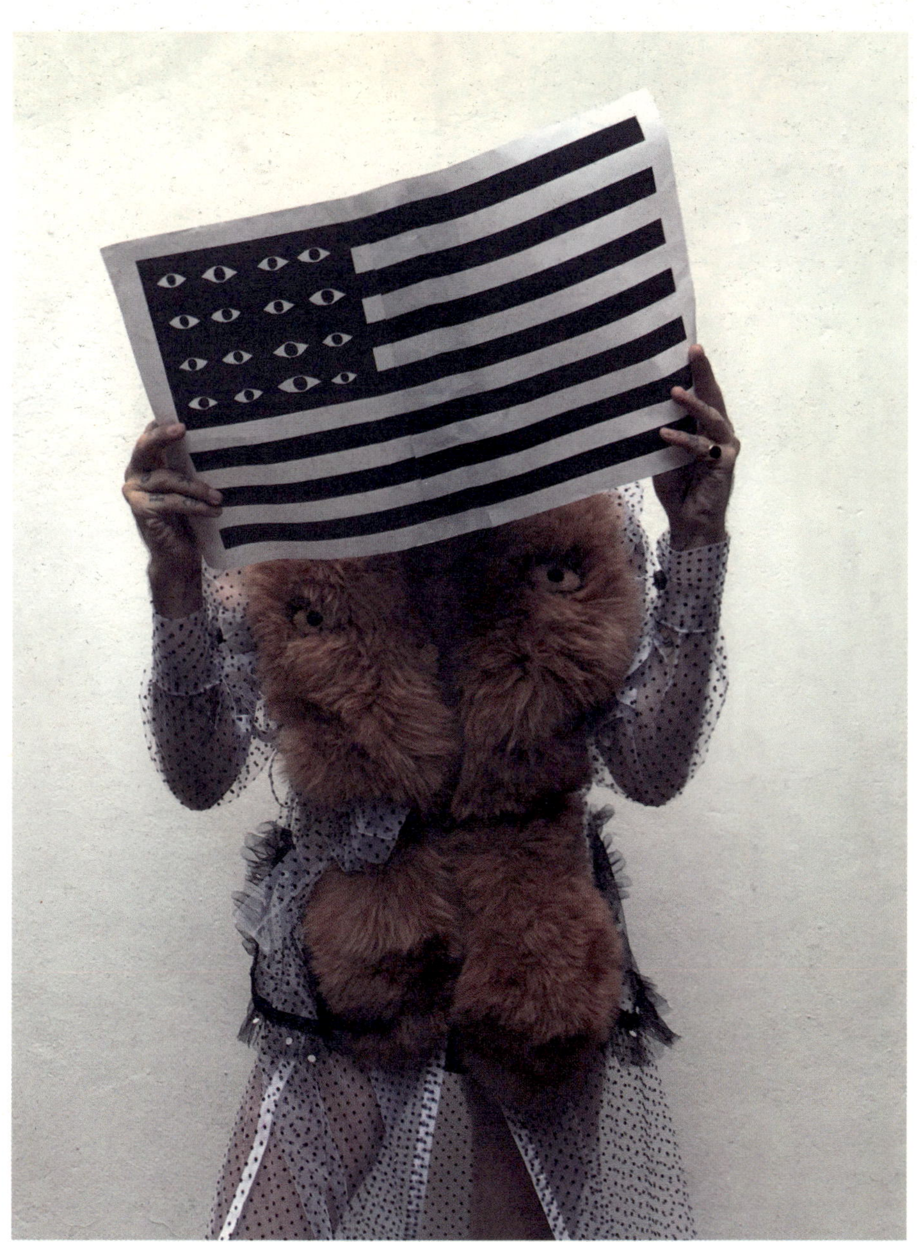

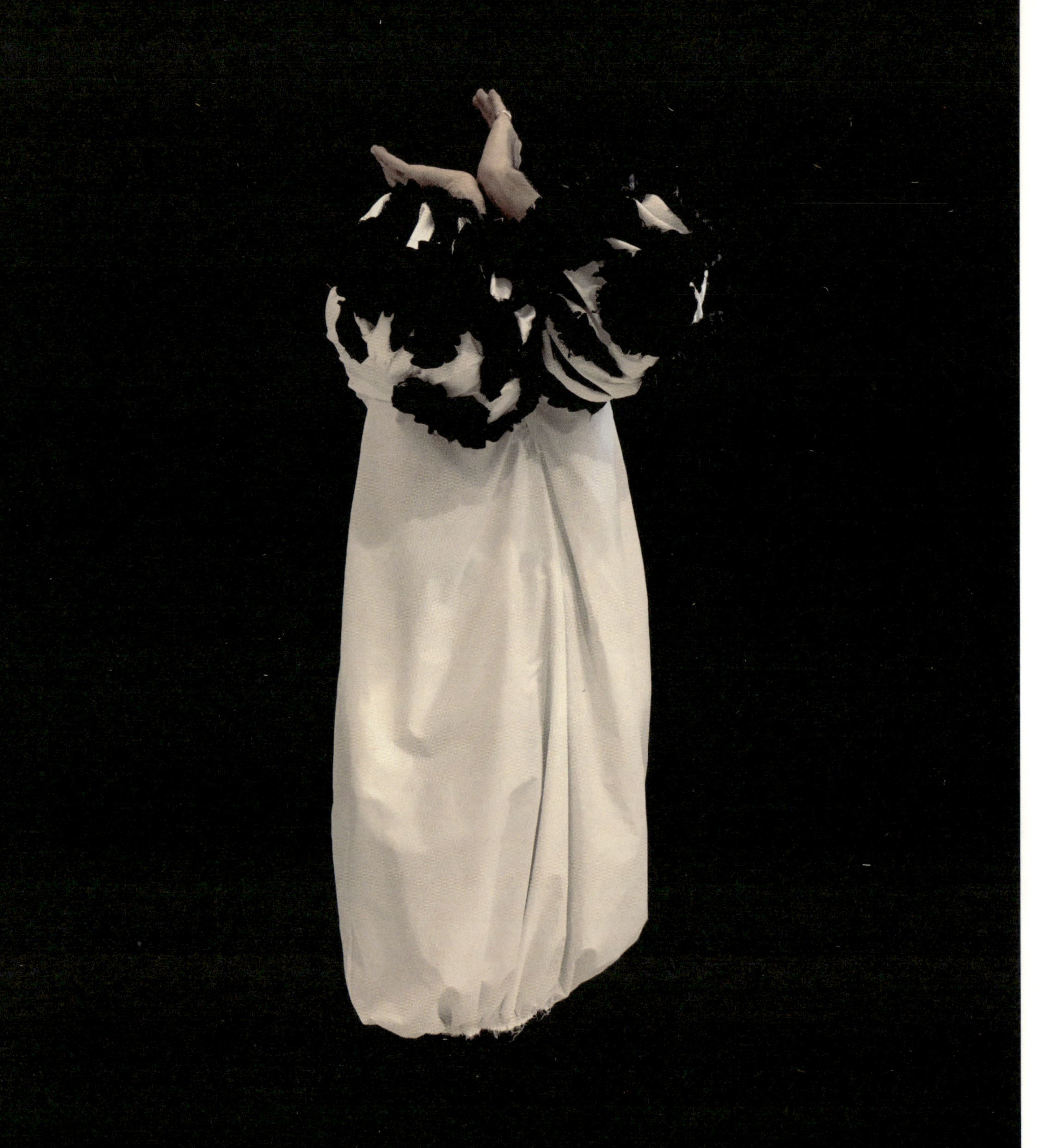

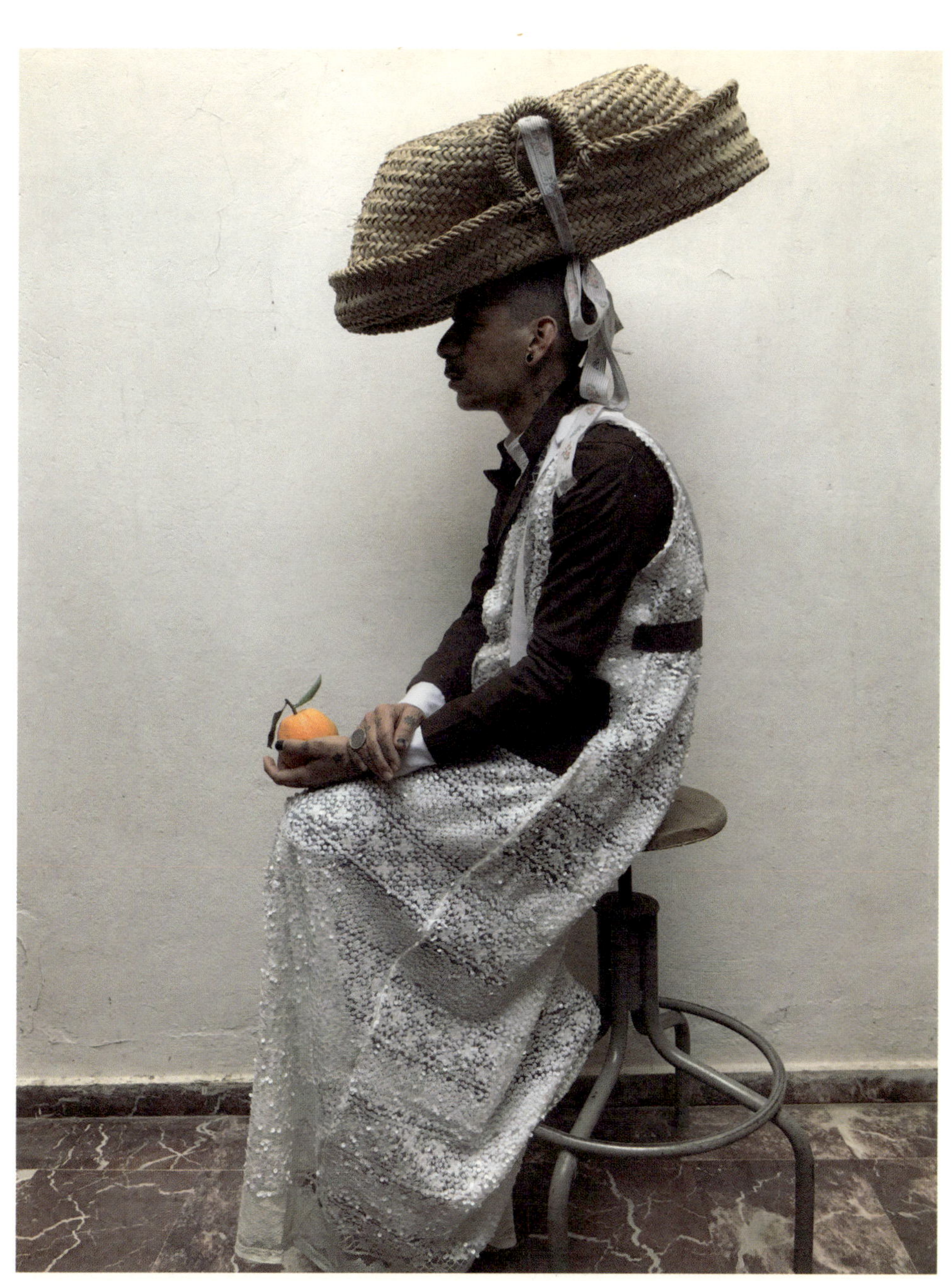

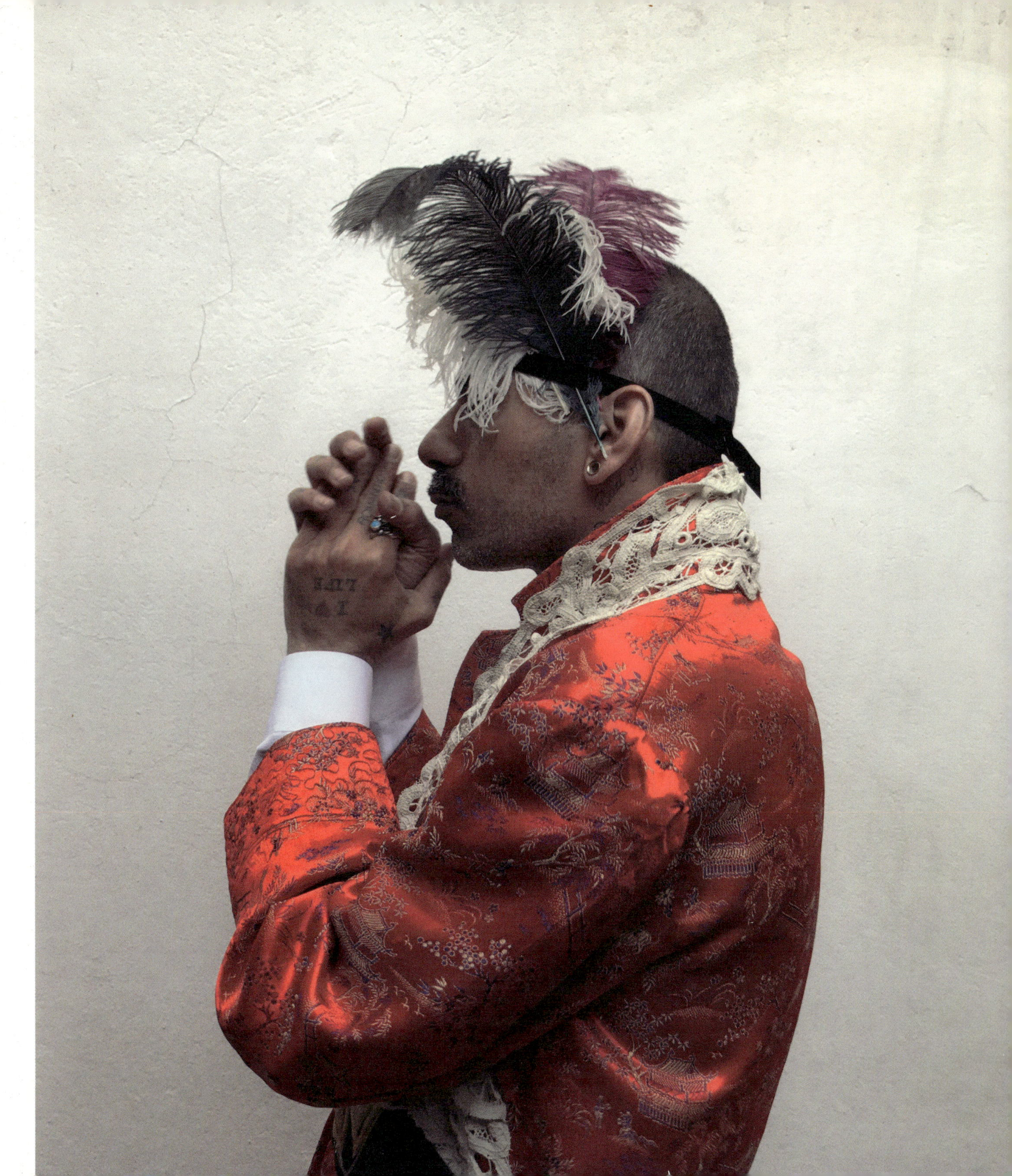

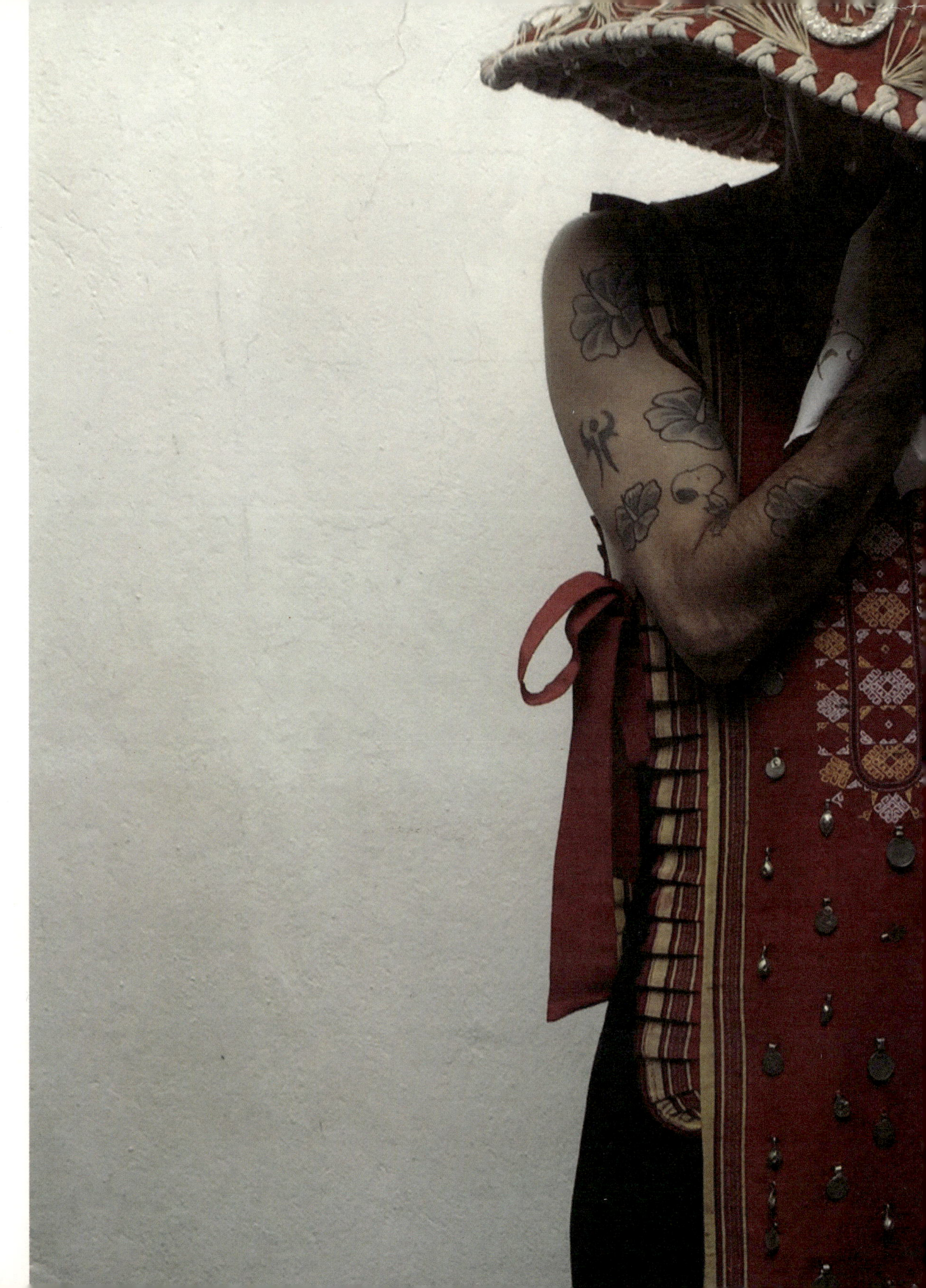

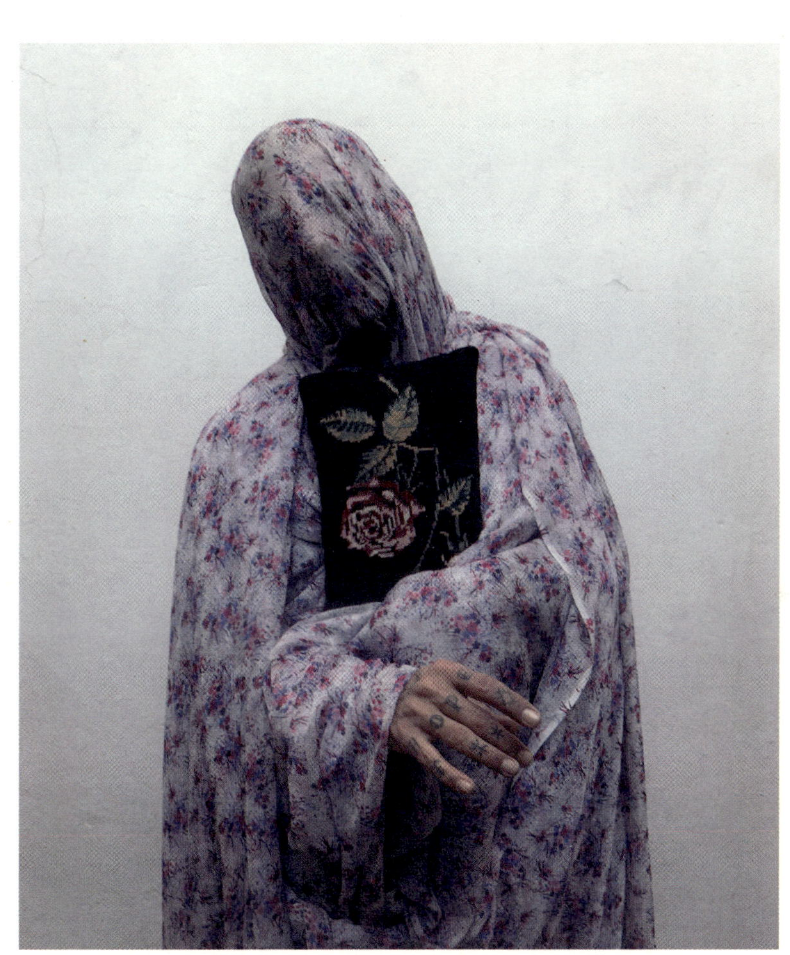

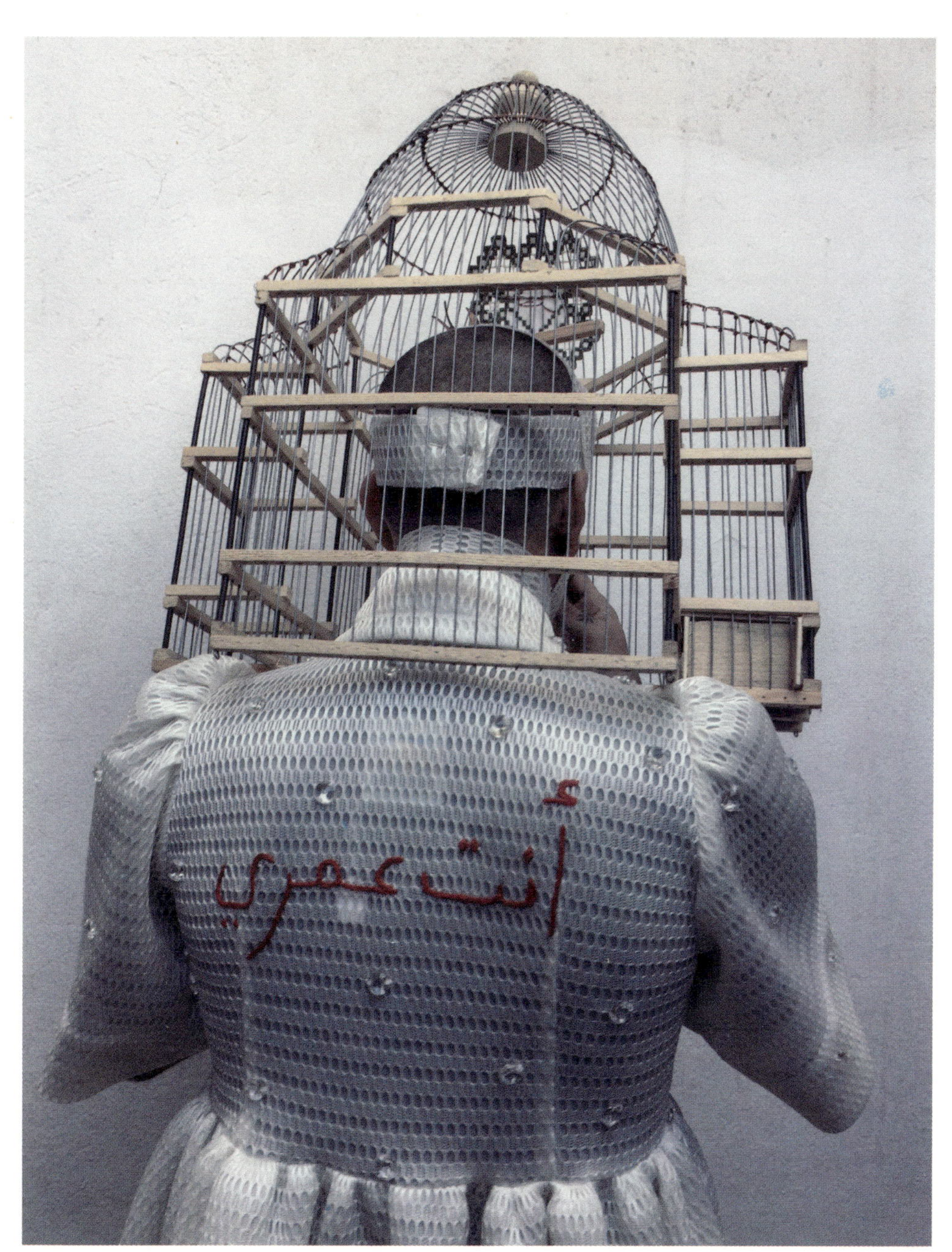
أنت عمري

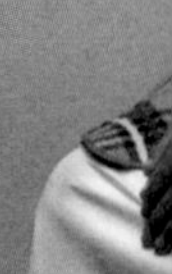

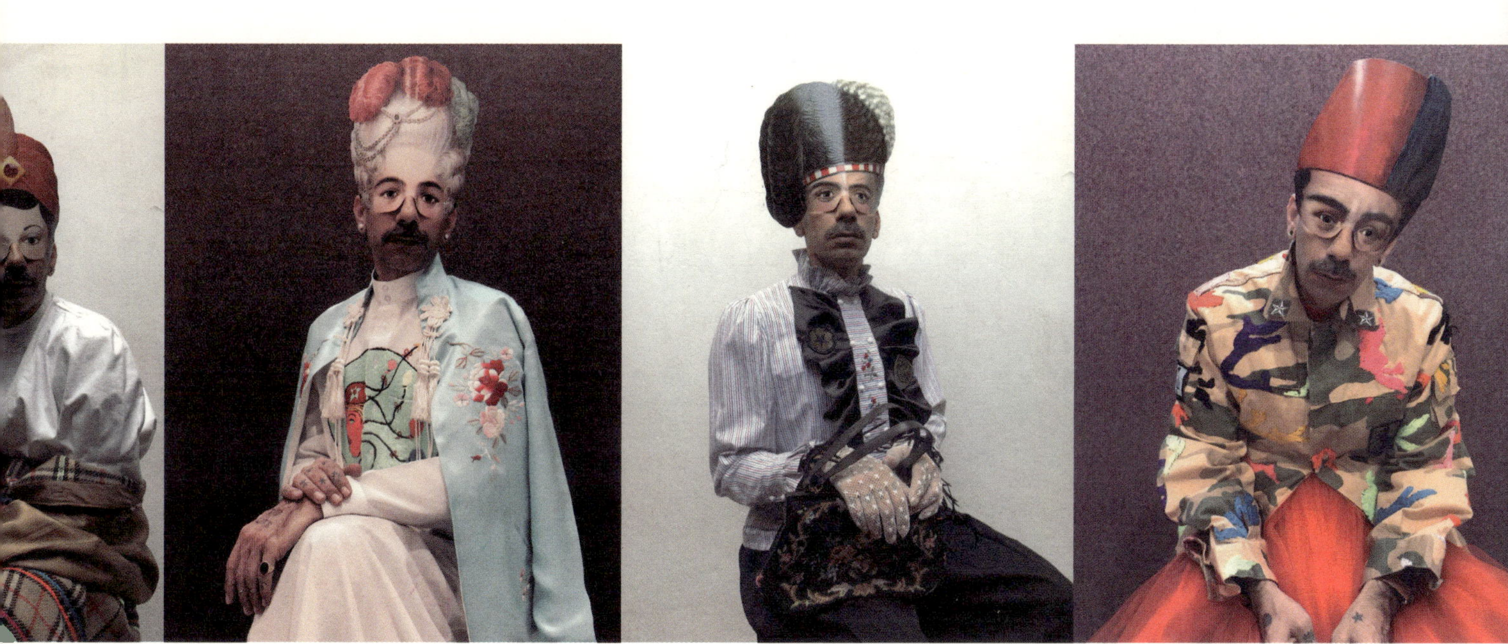

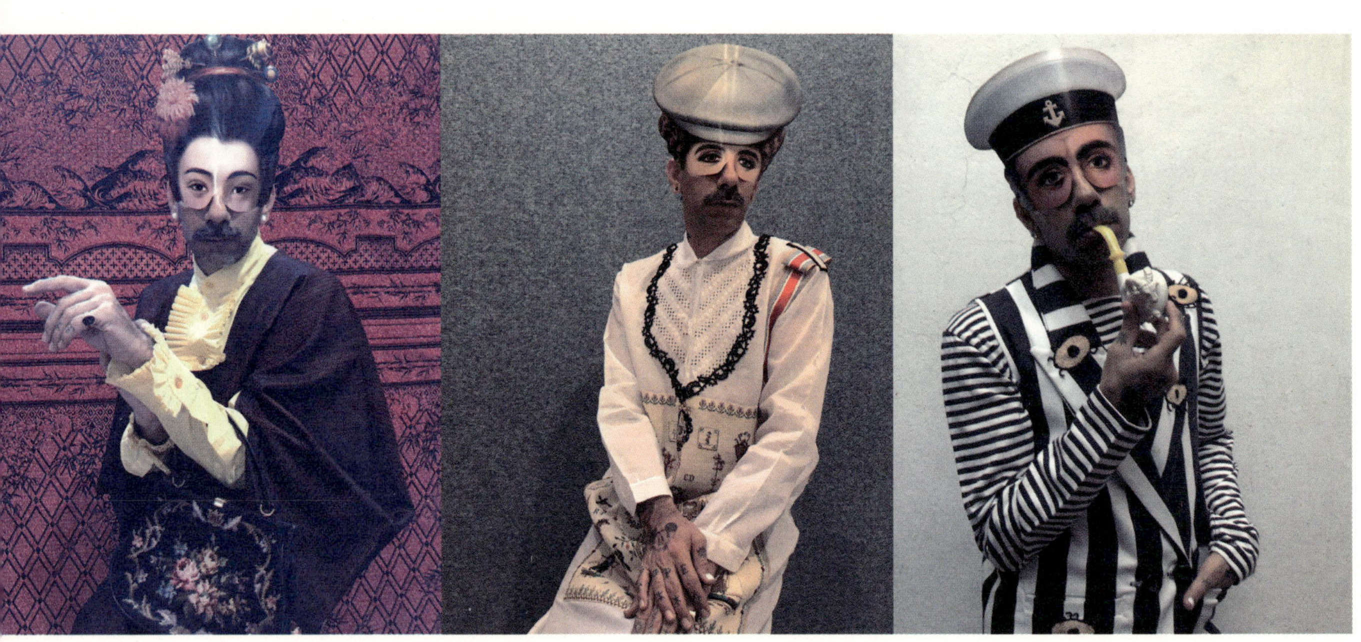

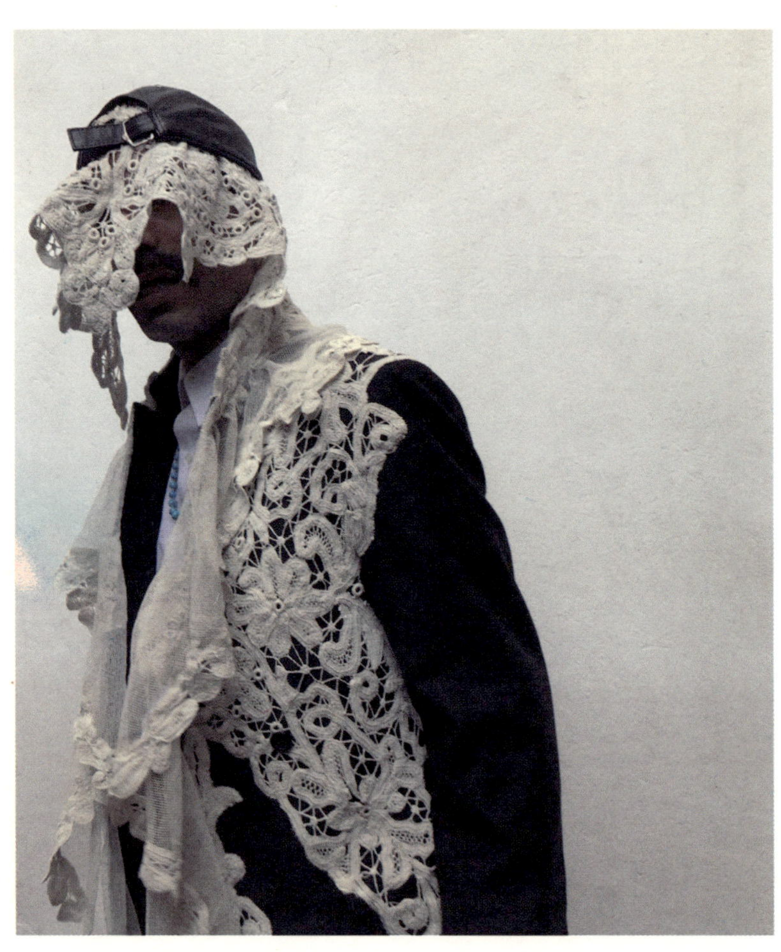

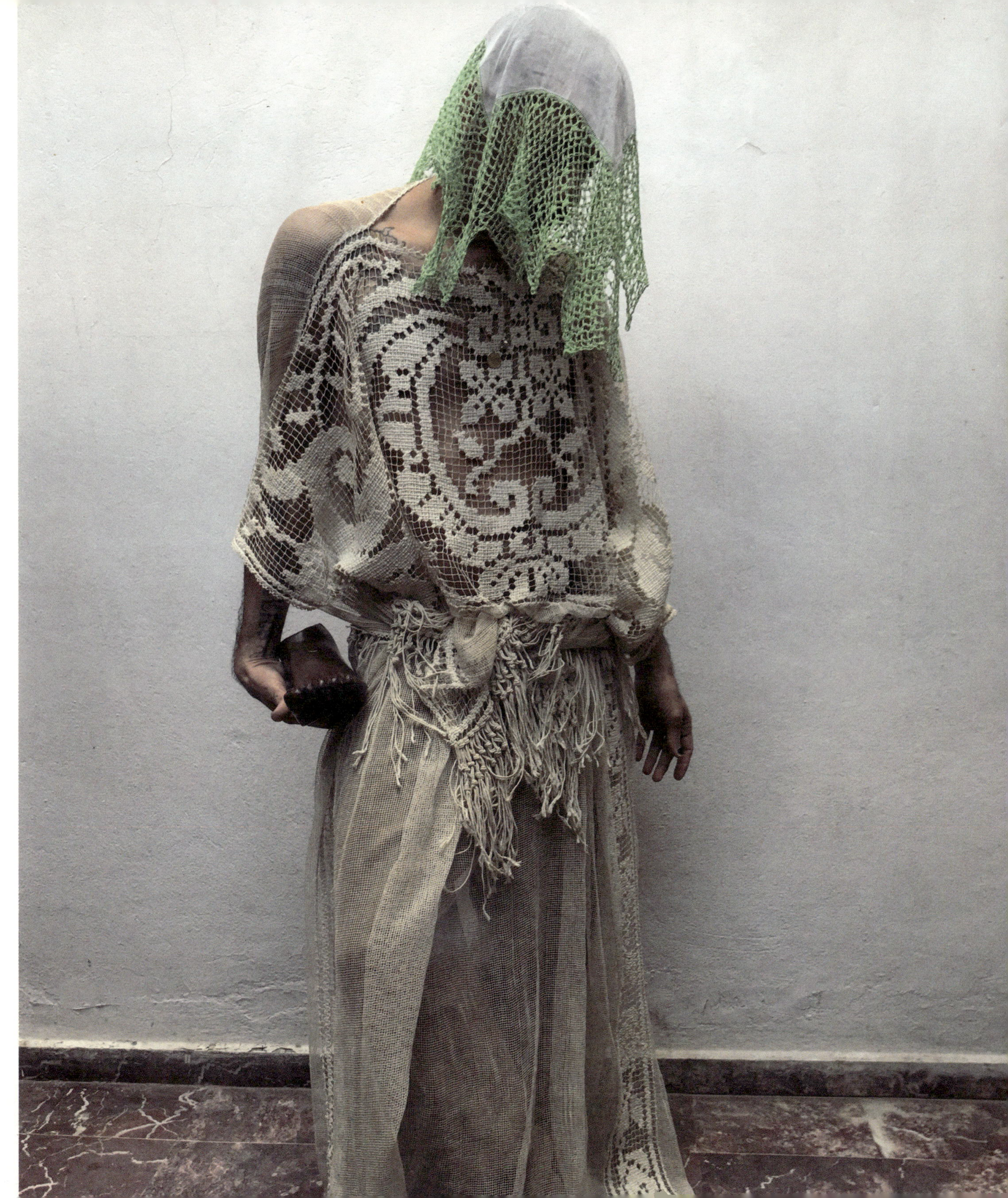

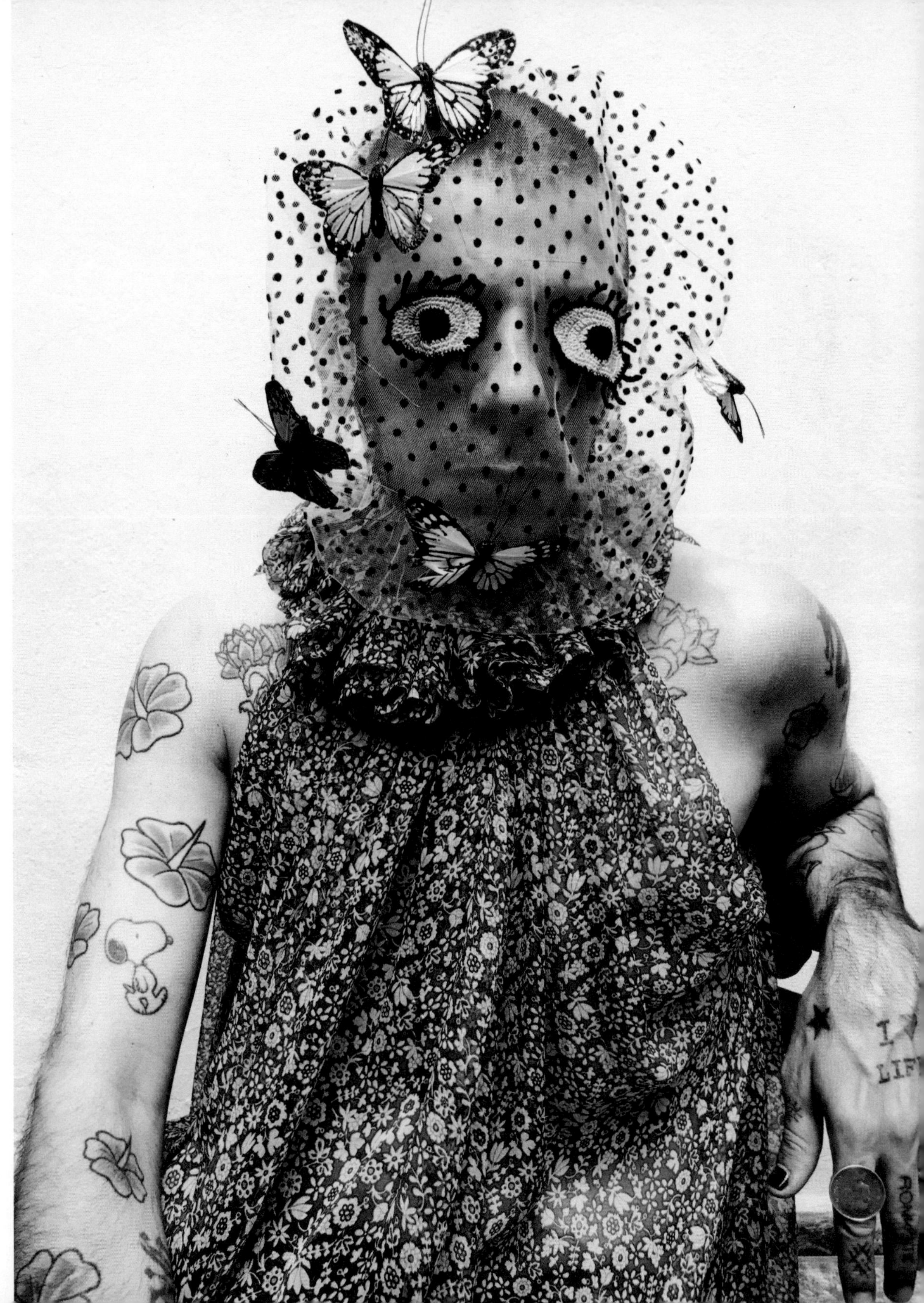

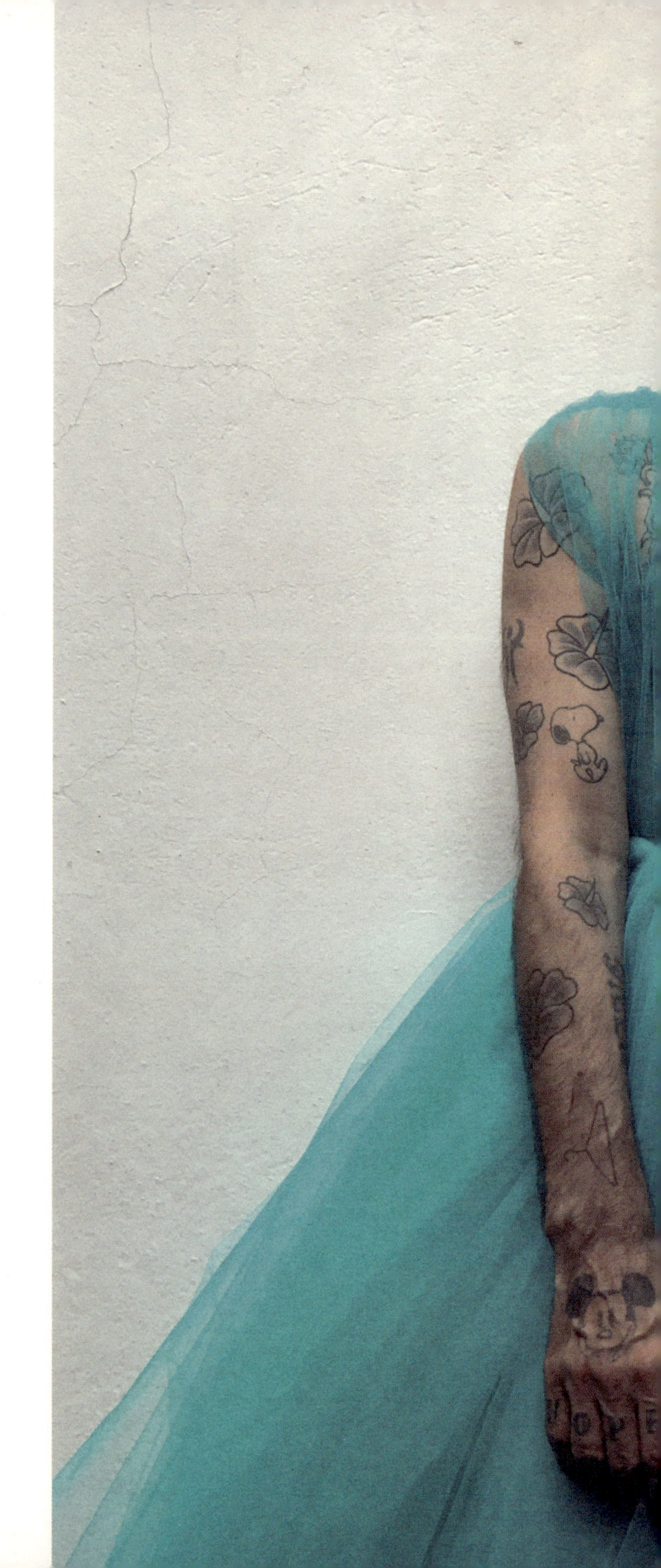

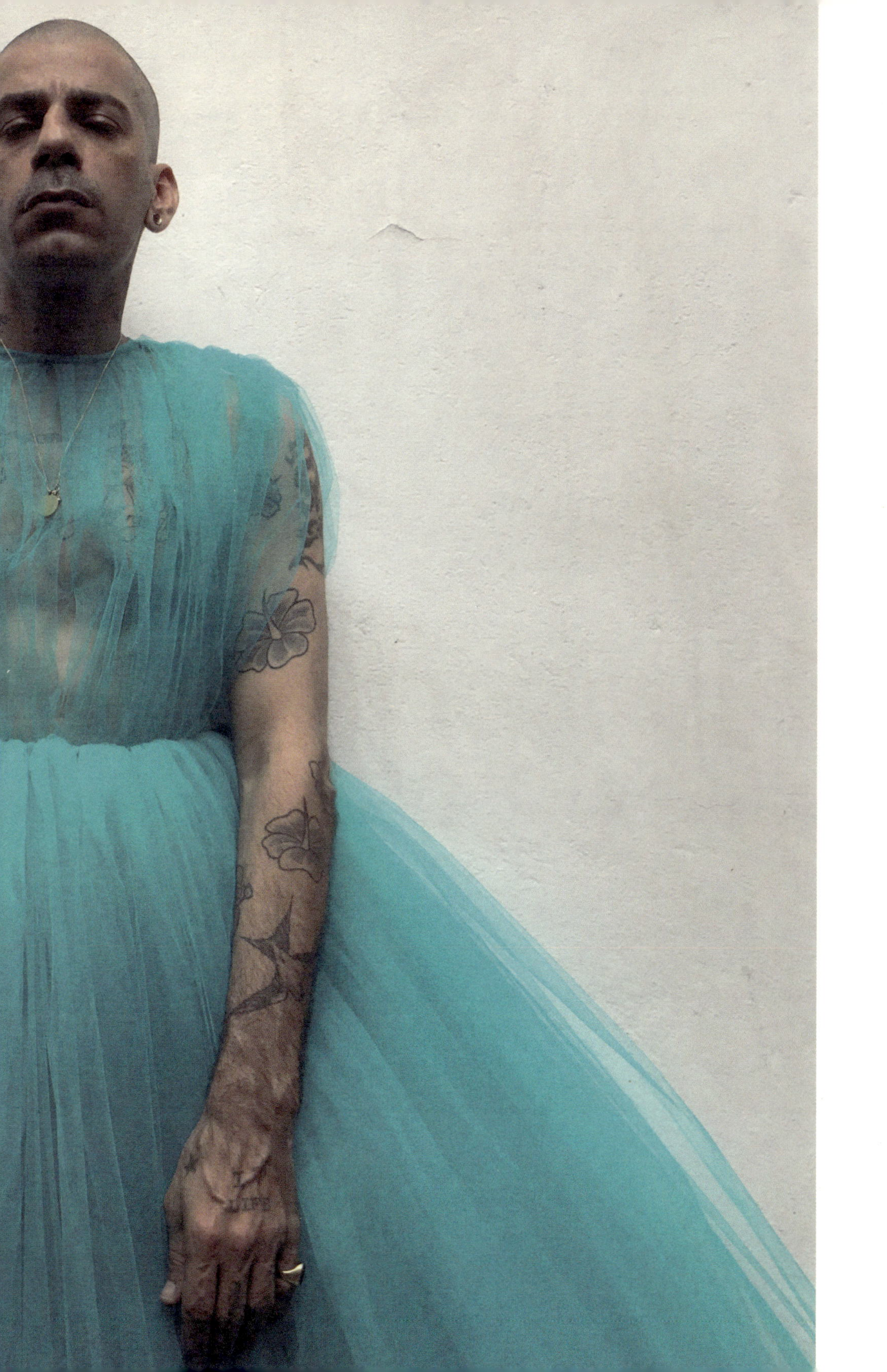

Rinat Aboulafia

Artsi, let's play a game. Maybe you'll have to take your shirt off, maybe not. Metaphorically, I think that your tattoos – which nobody can ignore as they are all over your body, make a sort of map.

They are beautiful. Can you tell me a little bit about some of them?

Then you have the LOVE tattoo. Do you think HOPE is stronger?

Are you the kind of man that knows how to let go?

TThat wasn't the question. You know how to let down, to let up, to let on, and to let go?

Going back to the tattoos, you are showing them in your pictures, yet often you're hiding your face.

I think that, in a way, part of what you want to say with your storytelling in these pictures, is that you want people to understand that they can be whatever they want. And be glamorous as you are.

Like what?

Artsi Ifrach

It wasn't the intention in the beginning, but through time it has actually become a sort of map of my life. It also has to do with my work, as it symbolizes the way I feel about things. Each one has a different symbol and meaning and, of course, it's a decoration.

I think the most obvious one is Mickey Mouse, which is actually the most recognizable one. Mickey Mouse means different things to me. First of all, it represents the child in me, which hopefully I will always be. Then I think of him as my eternal boyfriend. He's always smiling, making me feel happy. He is a great icon and he is timeless as I would like my work to be.
Under Mickey Mouse I have the HOPE tattoo. Hope is a strong word, as its definition means the continuation of something positive coming ahead.

I do have the love. Love and hope are equal. I start everything with love and end everything with love. I do also have HOLD ON, which reminds me, every time I'm facing crises, to tell myself, "OK, you should hold on". At the same time, on my feet, I have LET GO, as while I'm holding on, I also do have to let go. I can hold on many things that are important to me, but you got to let go the less important ones, if you want to make the whole thing, in a way, much easier.

I don't know what kind of man I am, but I definitely try to be a good one.

I'm trying all the time.

I'm dealing with something that has to do with personality, with what some people call costume, outfit, culture. They all go together and I hide my face to allow them to look at it freely. I don't want my face to look at them. I got something on me that might touch them, so I'm trying, through the pictures, to have them look at themselves. And hopefully provoke something into their memories. I'm playing a lot with that.

I don't think that people should be glamorous as me. I don't consider what people think when I'm actually doing it. I just let it go and the minute it's out, it does not belong to me anymore, it belongs to the person who looks at it. How people will feel about it, I don't know. I just hope it will provoke something in them. The pictures are supposed to create, to awake something.

Like memories. Like hope, love, beauty, struggle, dreams. This is why we take pictures.

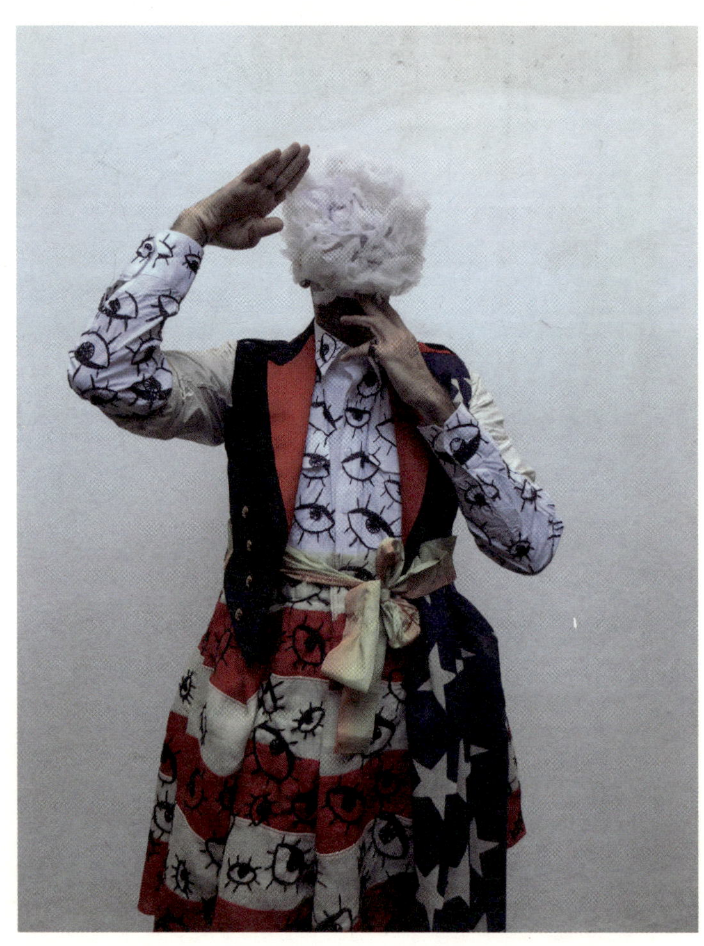

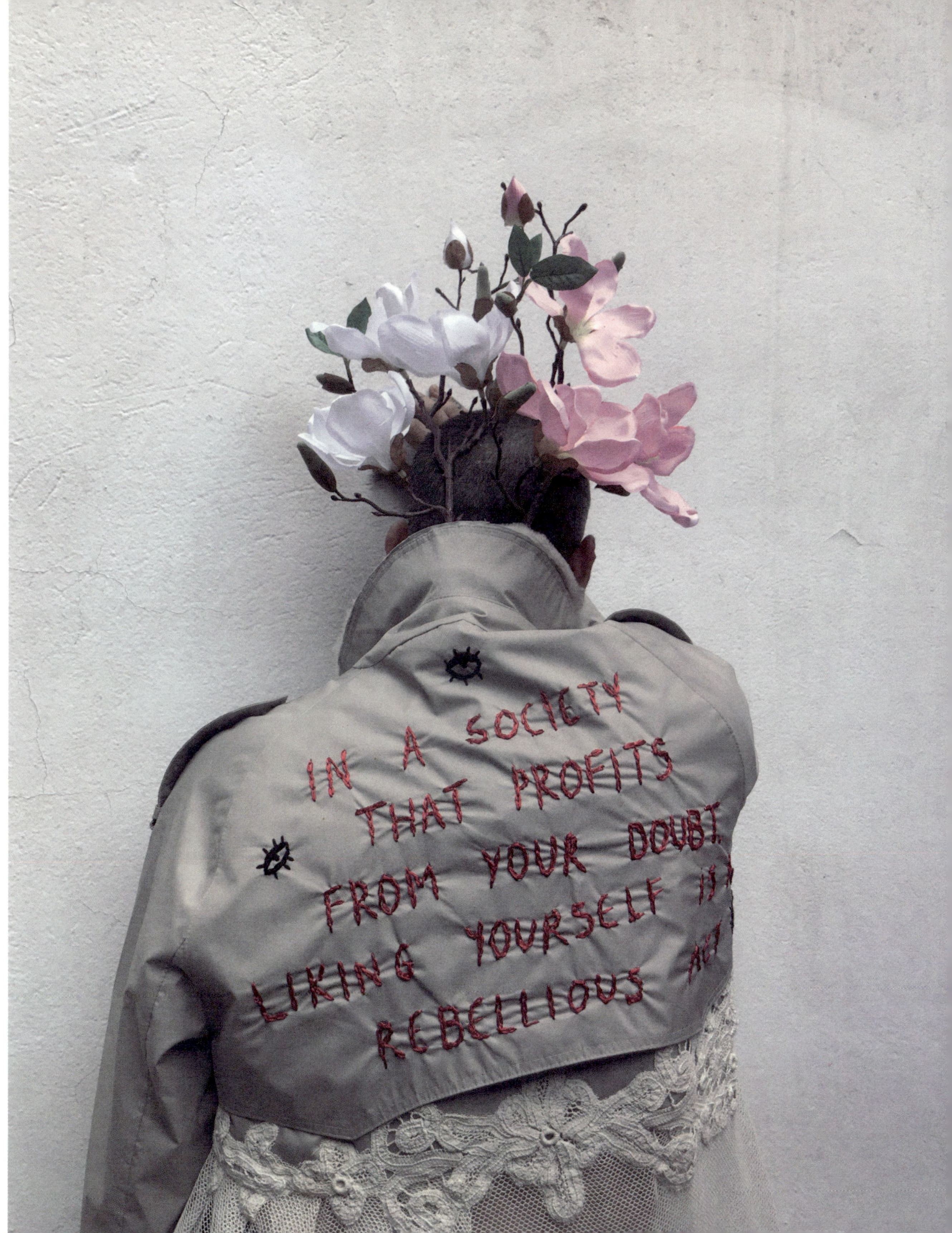
IN A SOCIETY
THAT PROFITS
FROM YOUR DOUBT.
LIKING YOURSELF
REBELLIOUS

Rinat Aboulafia

Speaking of memories. Your creations are made of memories. Using vintage means dealing with the past. I want to know a little bit about your memories. Like the first time you touched fabric.

Do you appear in your pictures as an actor?

So, who is in the center? Is it you, your garments or the character you are playing?

Actually, talking about this reminds me the first time I saw you. It was in Marrakech, during the Ramadan. It was a very hot day and I was sitting at the "Café des Épices". The "Herb's one", the "Spiced coffee". It was a beautiful place.

Everybody goes there, right?

You came in the café and I couldn't take my eyes off you. You were so different from the rest. You were wearing a huge hat with a beautiful djellaba. And now we are sitting in Hotel Grand Amour in Paris, two Israelis breaking their teeth in English, which is not their mother language. Although you speak English most of the time, right?

Let's go back to the beginning, because you are made of different cultures. You were born in Jerusalem, then moved to Tel Aviv, Amsterdam and back to Tel Aviv.

Artsi Ifrach

I do deal with memories a lot, as I think everyone does and differently. I'm trying somehow to fix my memory, whether I have a nice or a bad one, through my compositions, my pictures.

My first memory about garments is with my drama teacher. I was very young, and I used to go to her house. There was a huge wooden box with inside a lot of costumes. It was her teaching tool. I had to become different personalities and try to act something. Every time I had to open that box it felt like having a bunch of new options, possibilities, to be whoever I wanted to be. This has been my first approach to garments. Their value, make me handle them in the right way. I'm playing with them like an actor and his script, reinventing myself and changing all the time.

Of course.

Whoever you want it to be. I'm just the tool inside these garments, I'm the person who wears them. I created a sort of memory, a character, an image with one-of-a-kind piece. When you do one-of-a-kind piece, you can do that every day. You realize there are timeless possibilities. Well, not timeless, endless.

Yes, the "Café des Épices". It still a beautiful place.

Well, it's a landmark.

Yes, I do. I travel a lot, and I have lived most of my adult life outside of Israel, so it's the only way I can actually communicate.

Then Paris and finally Marrakech. In between, I went to New York, Tokyo, Germany. I am a traveller.

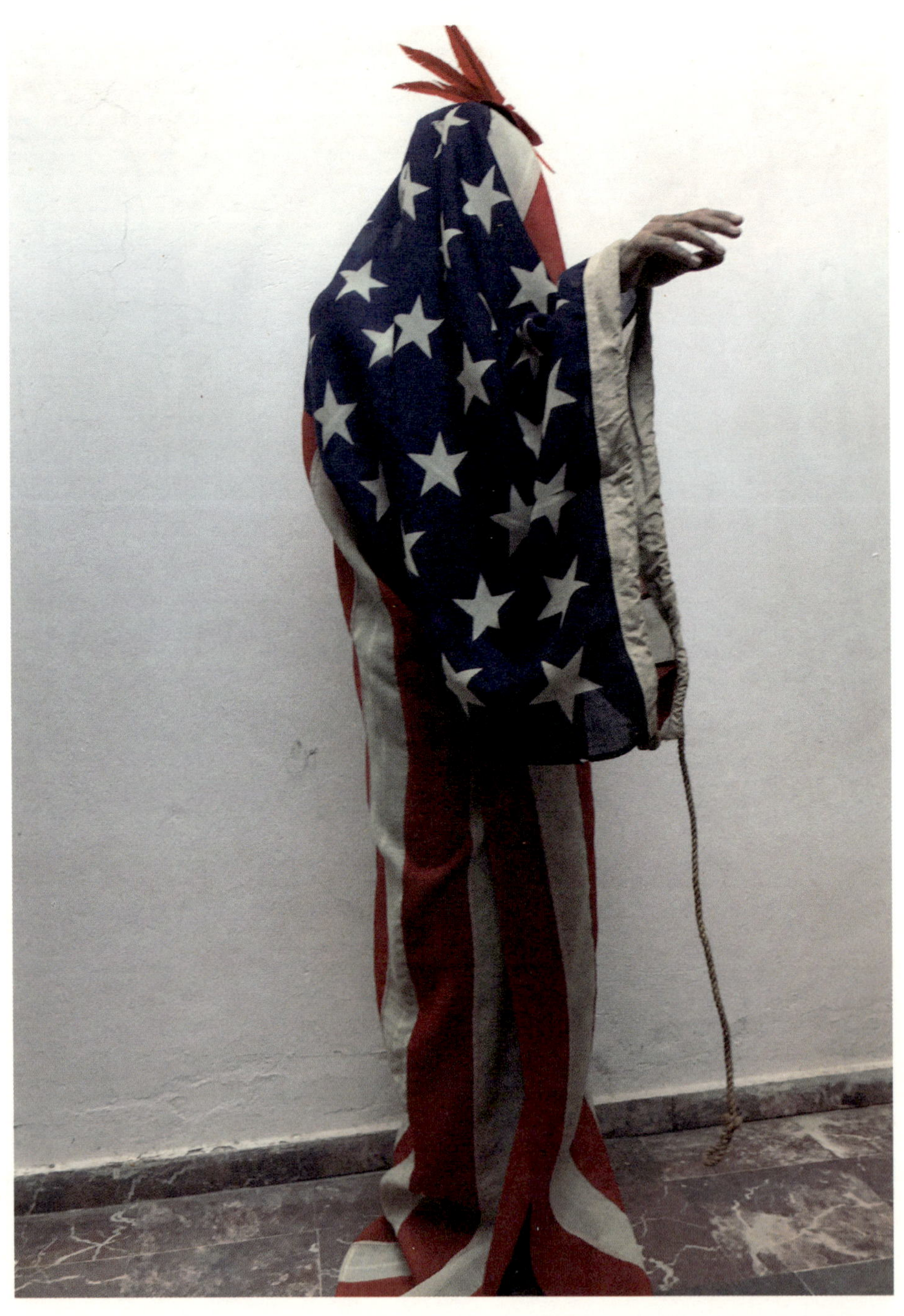

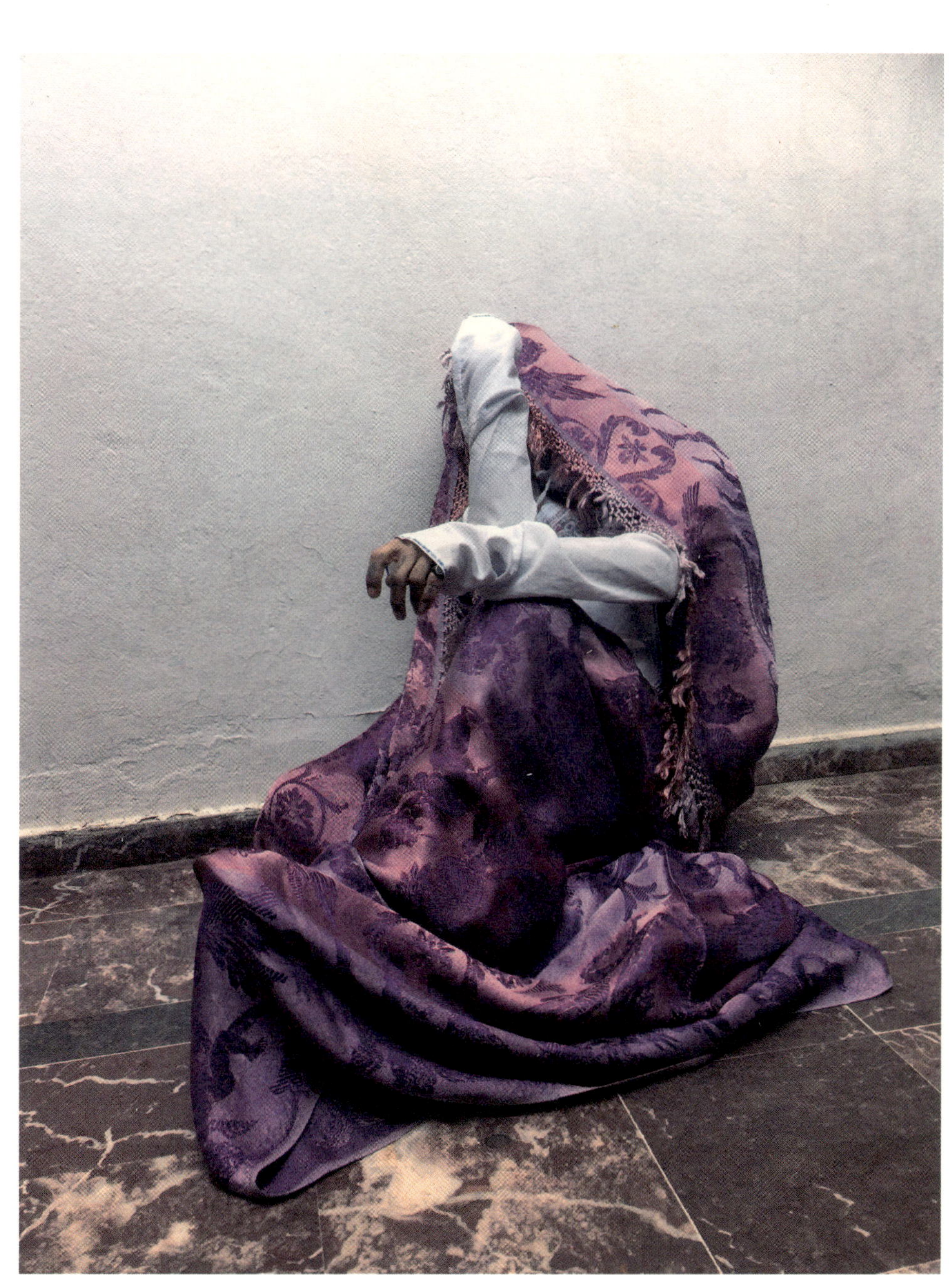

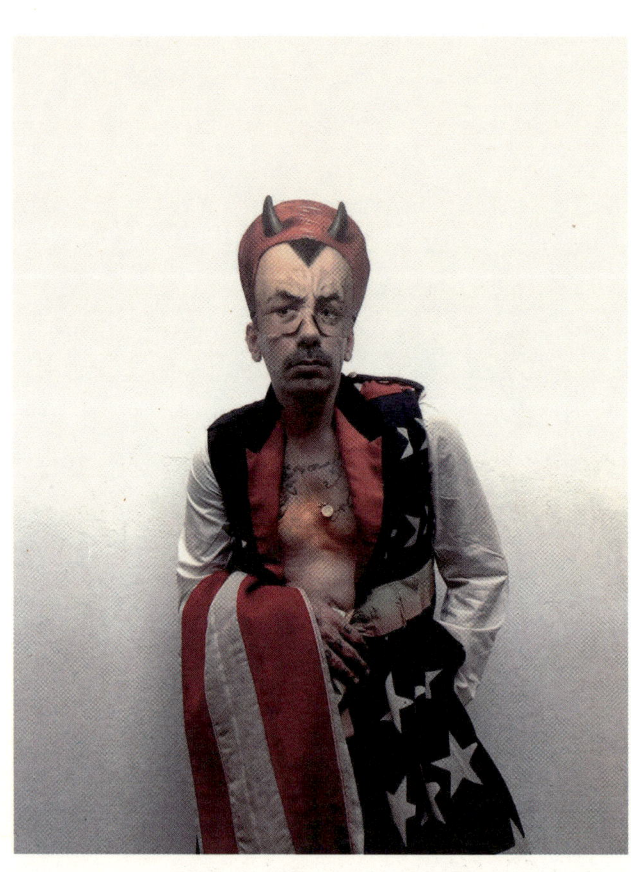

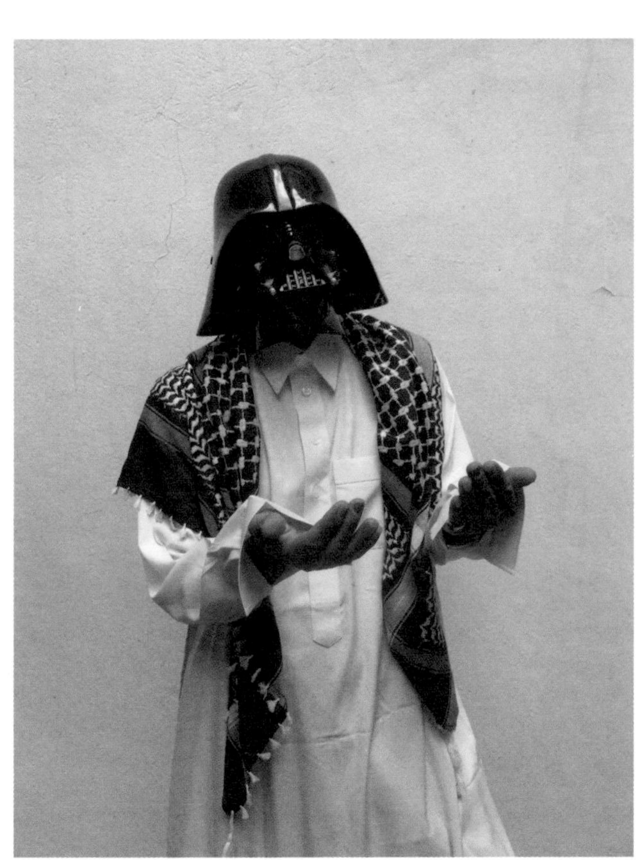

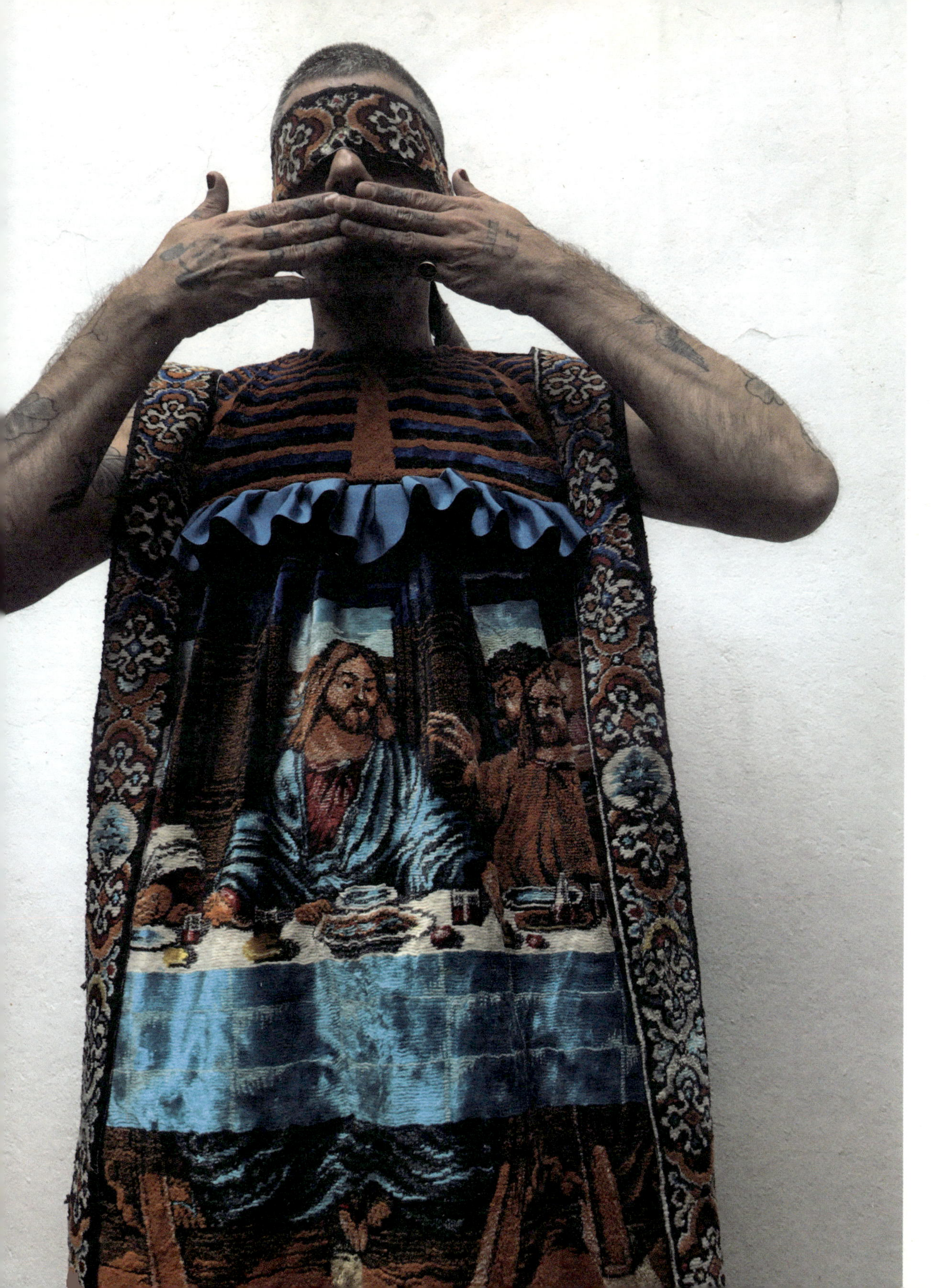

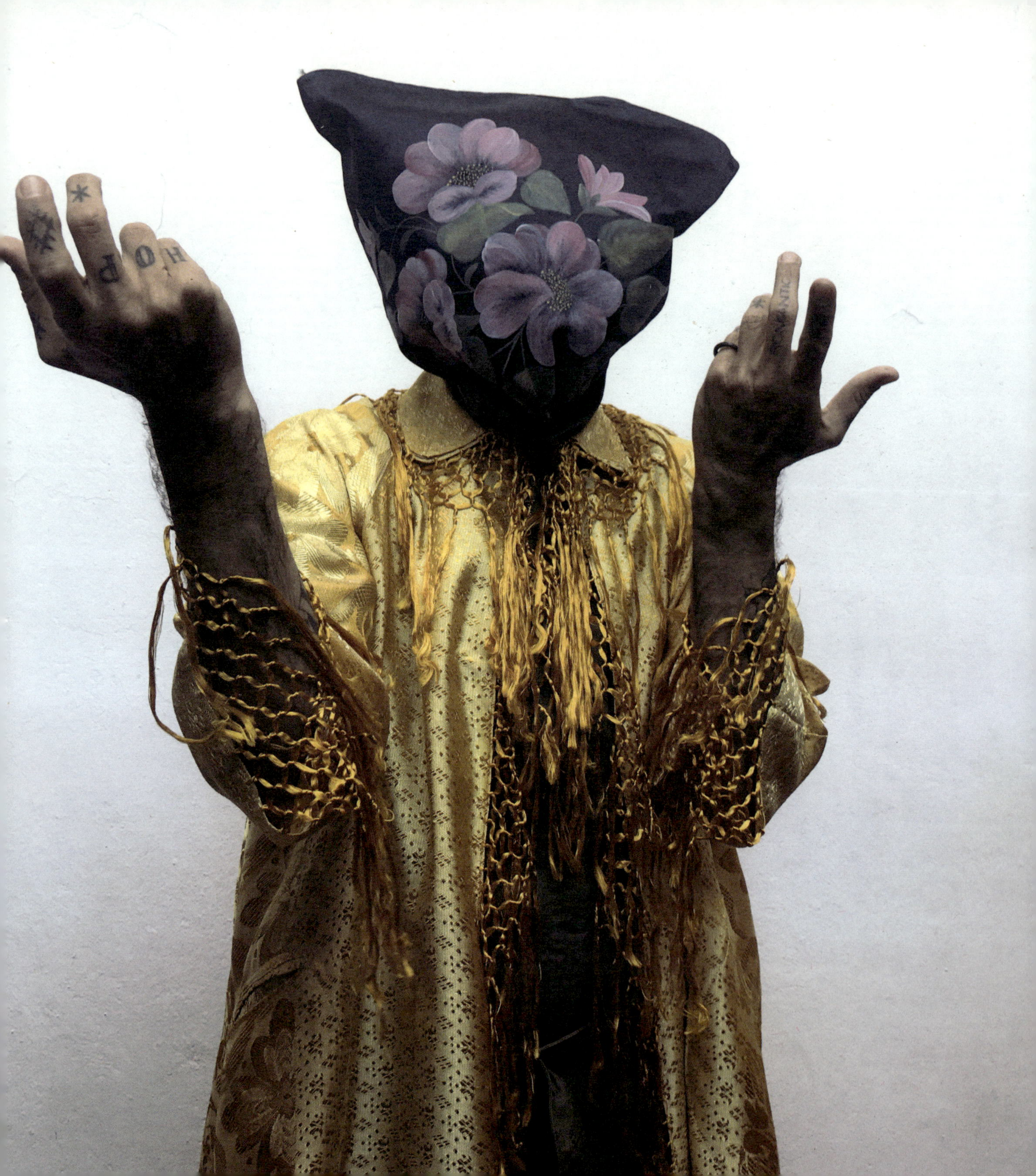

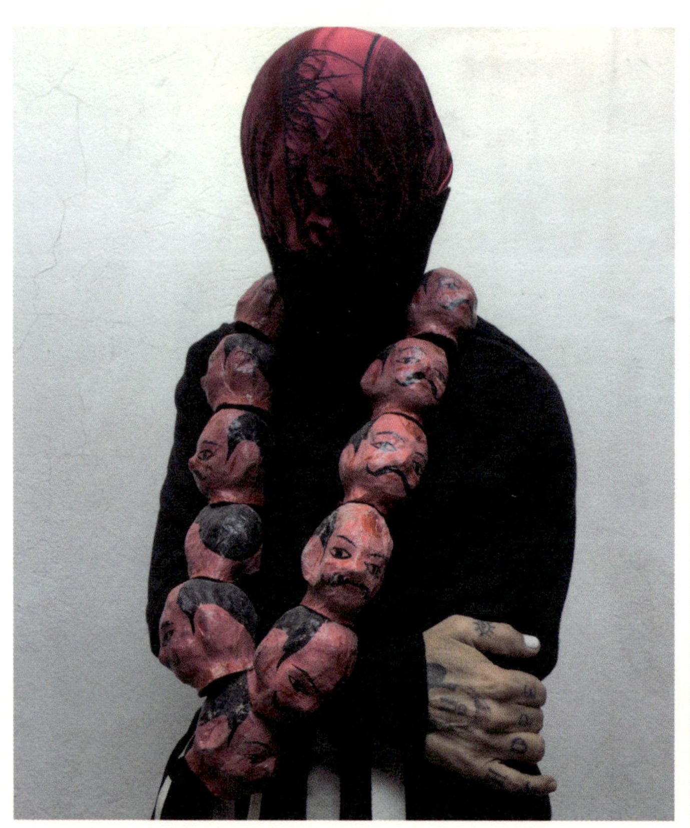

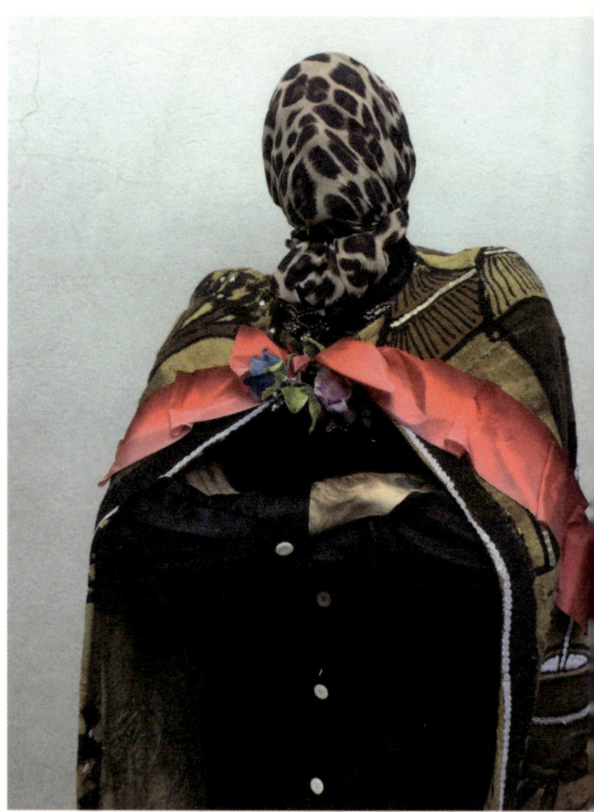

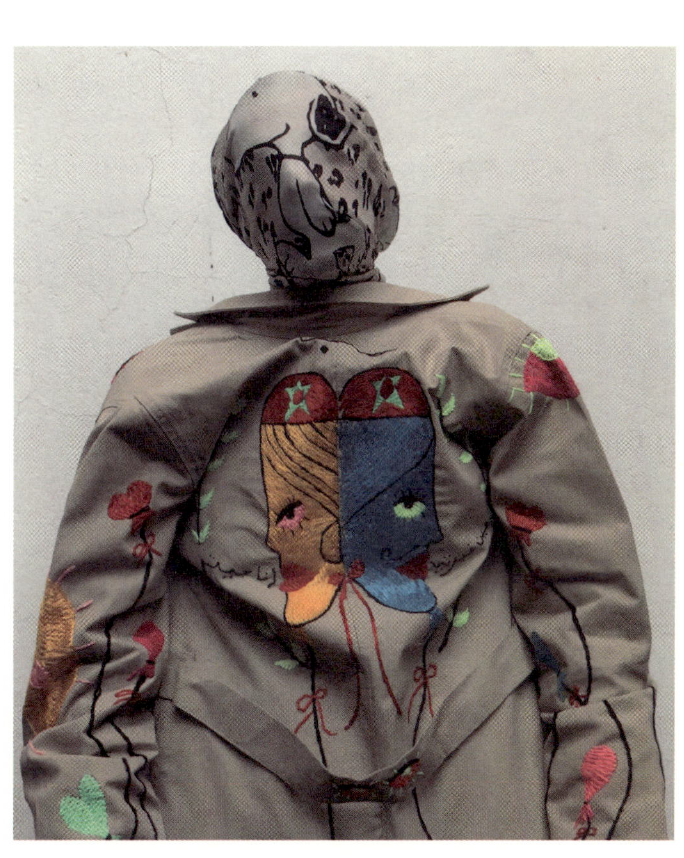

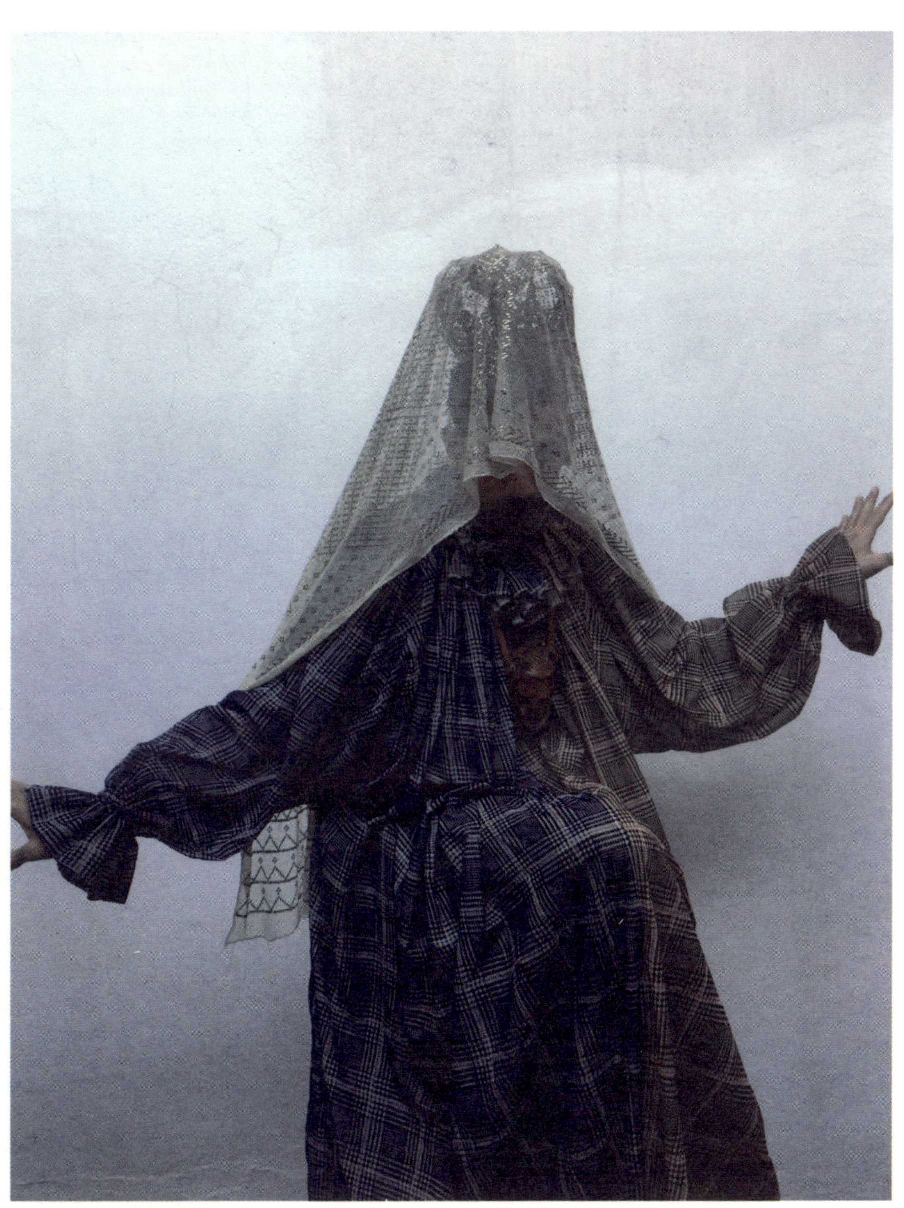

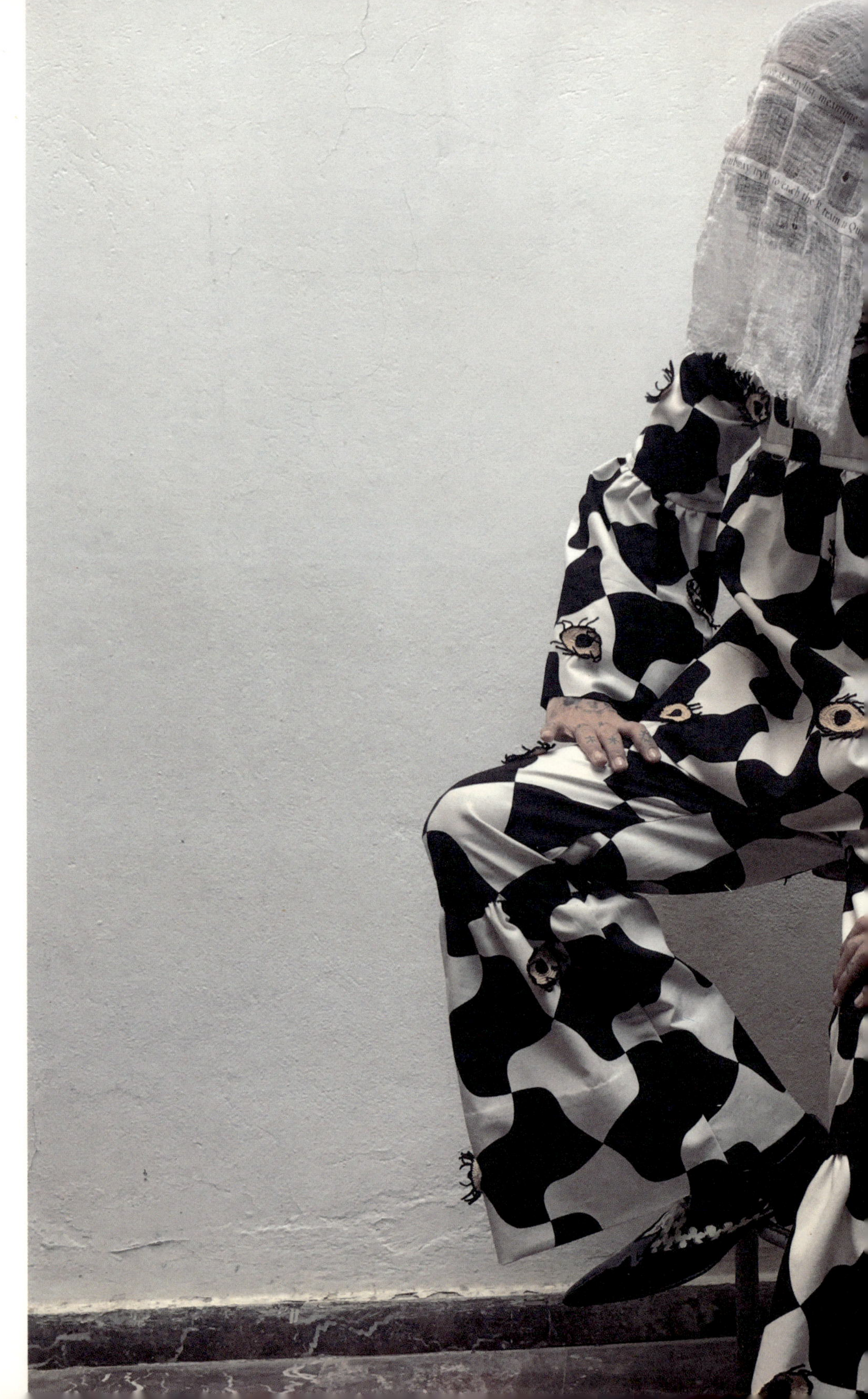

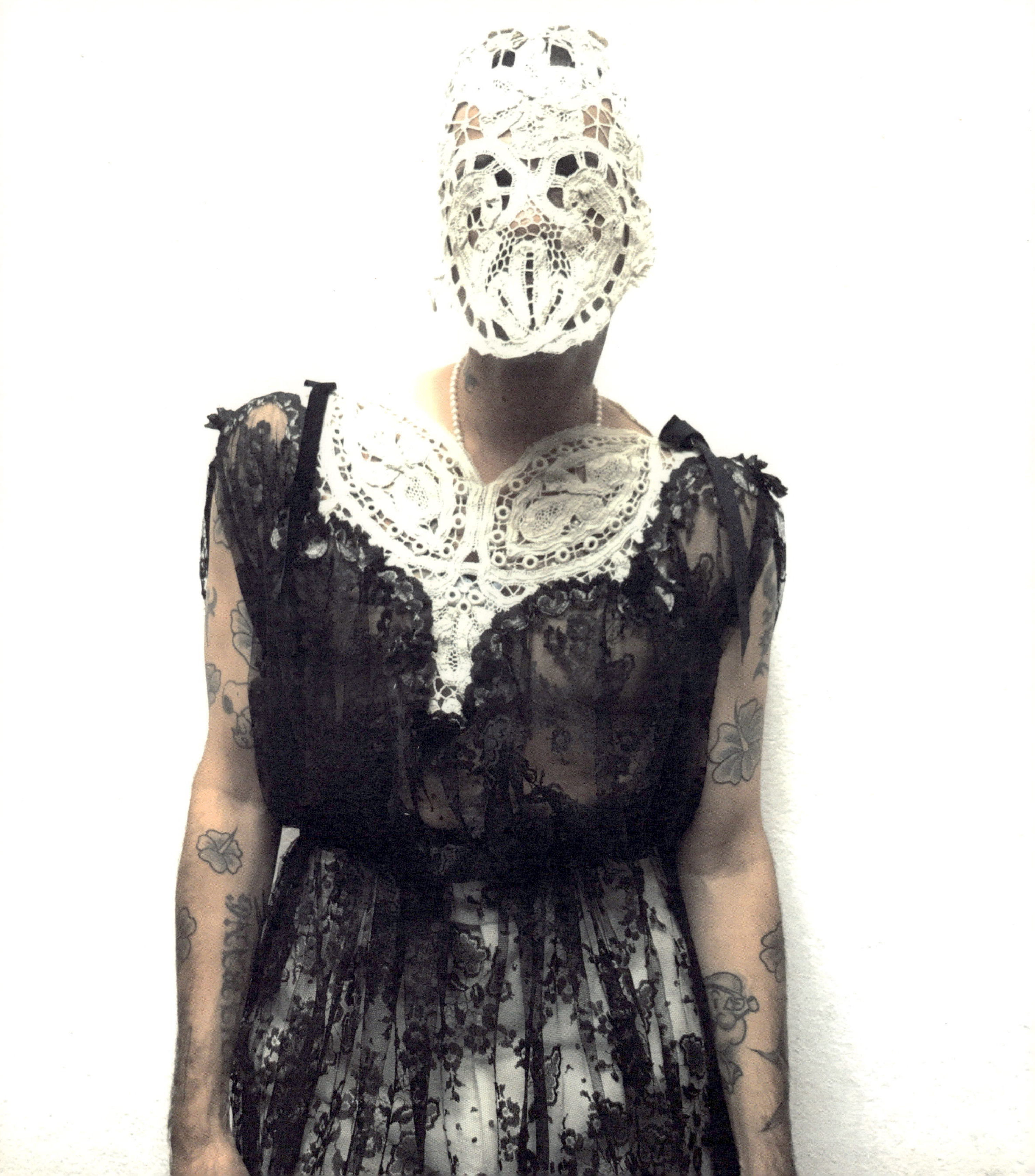

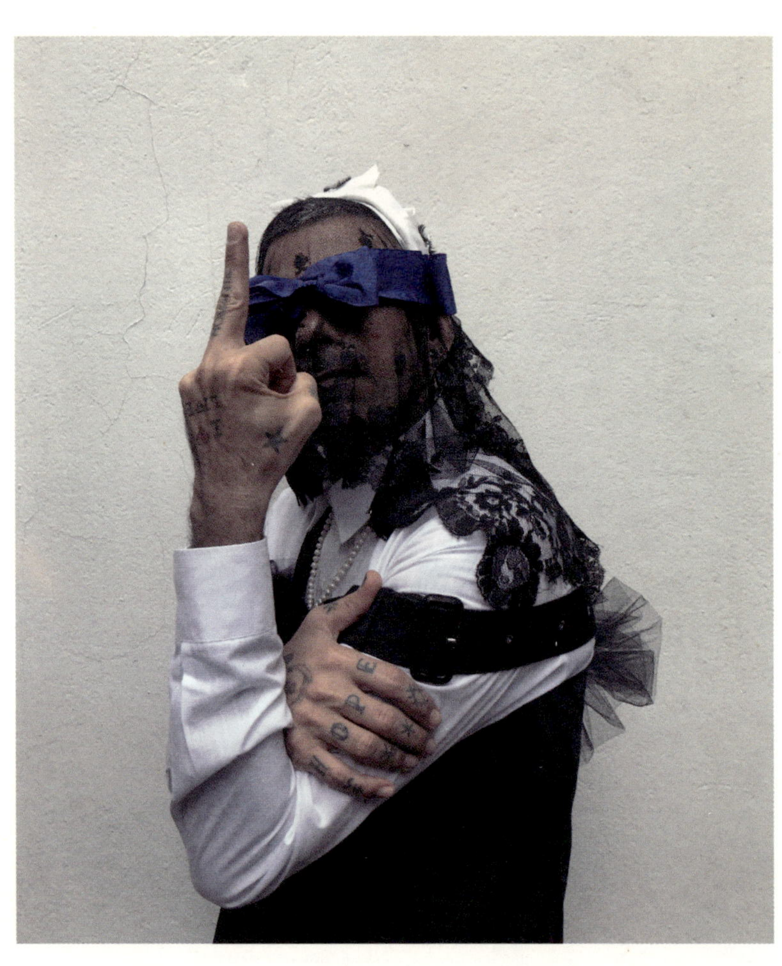

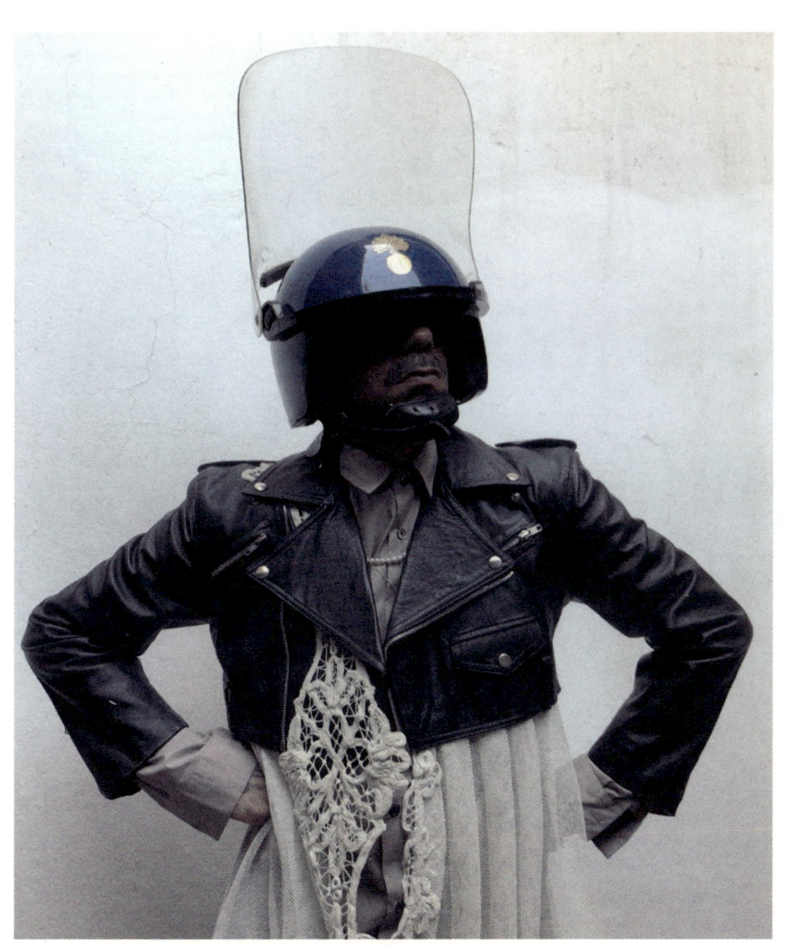

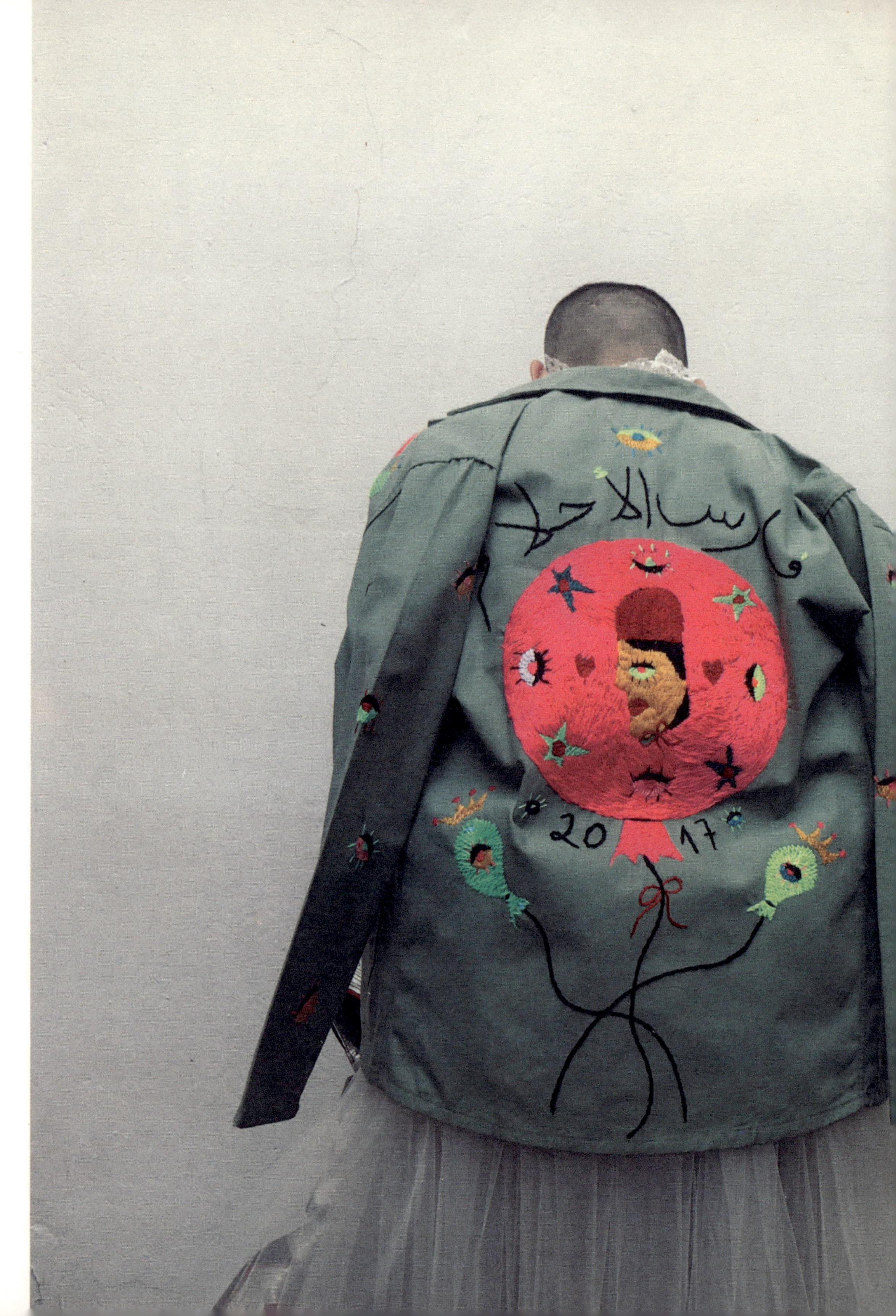
2017

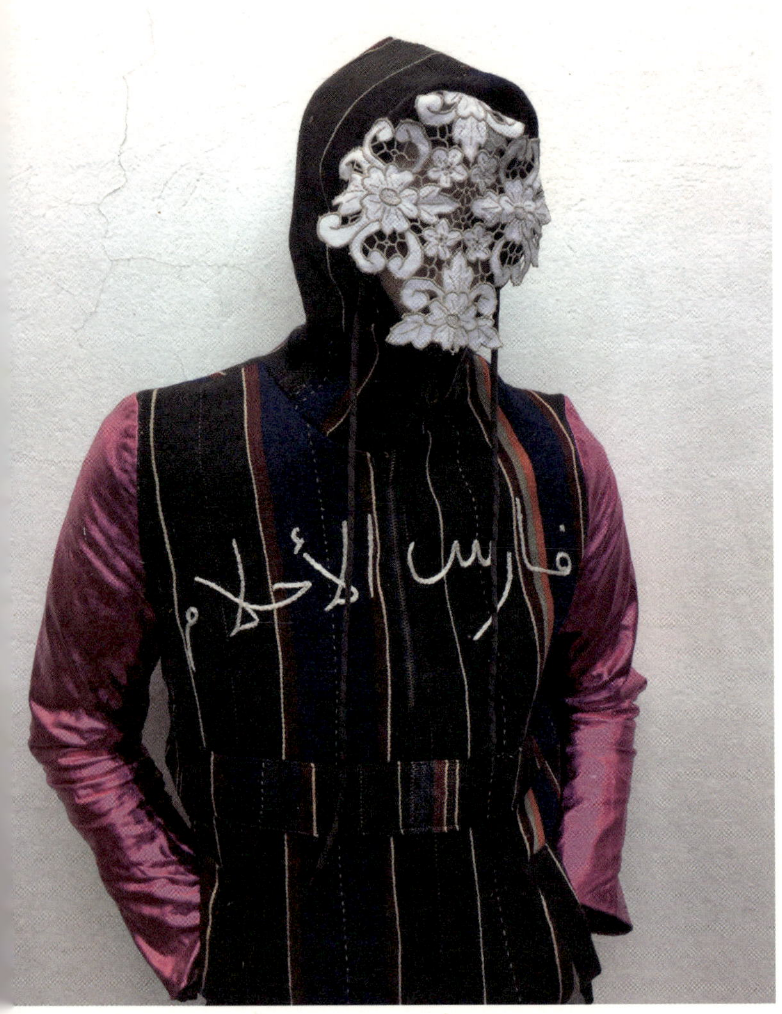
فارس الأحلام

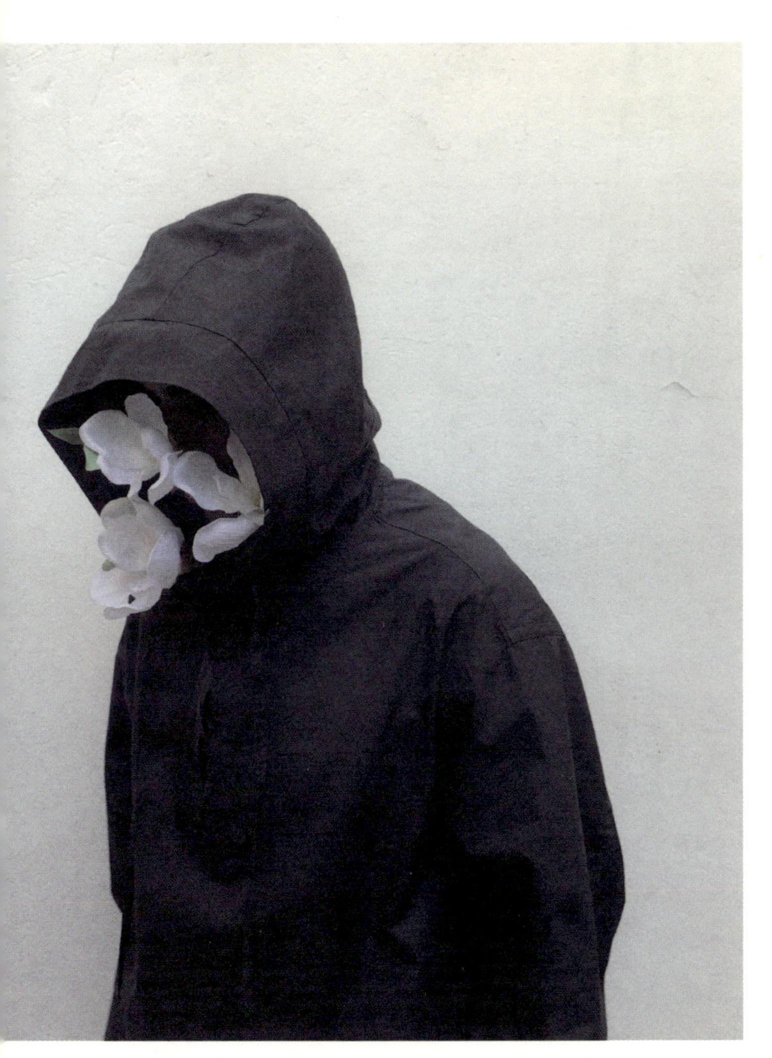

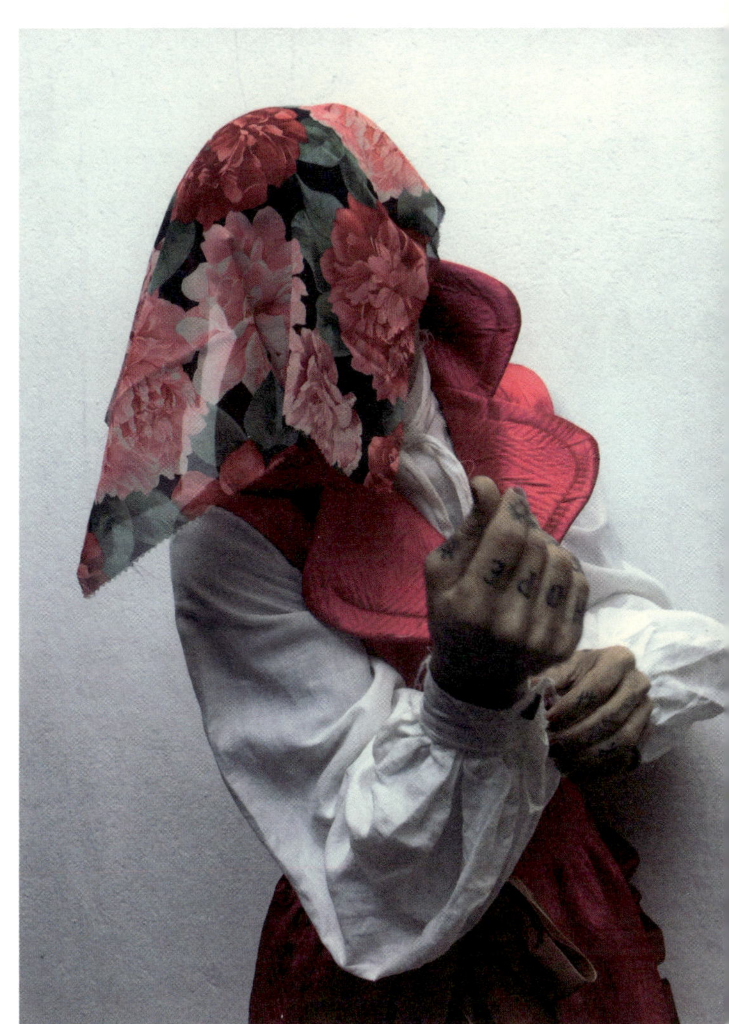

Rinat Aboulafia

How does this multiculturalism affect your work? Which culture has the biggest influence on you?

Everything about you is quite special and unique. You dye your hair blond and have a lot of tattoos. You were born in Israel as a Jew and you are now living as a gay man in a Muslim country. How do you deal with that in your everyday life?

Yes, I think about your work as crossing borders. Do you miss any of the places you left behind?

Yes, it also looks like magic. It seems to me that you are attuned to low and high frequencies. I can hear music coming from your work. Do you usually listen to music when you work?

Is there anything specific that you are listing to right now?

Artsi Ifrach

I think all of them matter. All the pieces I create come from existing pieces. I hardly ever use something new, I fix things, giving them a lot of respect. Some of them are museum pieces, in a way I'm committing a crime. But at the same time, I give them a new future and preserve the culture. I'm living in Marrakech where its culture lives on the street, which is rare, as in most of the other countries, their cultures are in museums.

I have a simple and more complicate answer to that. The simple answer is that I believe my energy creates everything. The complicate one is that I don't take it into consideration, but I do understand it's there and I have a lot of respect for the place I live in. I also have to say that my parents were born in Morocco, so I don't feel like I went to live in a Muslim country, I just went back home, trying to put back together and continue what my parents left behind. I do the same with my pieces. Jews and Muslims were always connected somehow. Politicians now put borders but I try to break those borders through my work.

I try not to. I don't like the word miss, because it means there is something missing in my life and I don't feel like that when I think of those countries. I always try to be in the place where I'm at the moment and move forward. As I said before I'm trying to fix memories. Every time I'm dealing with these missing places, I try to fix them by taking a picture, creating a piece connected to those cultures. Somehow it's therapeutic for me and it feels good. I don't know what I was in the past life, but I think there is so much information we don't use. So, I cannot give an answer to everything that has happened, I don't always understand the past, but suddenly the whole thing becomes magic.

Of course, I like Arabic and classic music. I used to be a dancer before, music influences the way I handle my clothes. It's again something that belongs to the stage. My work is my music, my movement, my way of dancing. I'm trying to put it all in one single image.

Yes, I am listening to a wonderful CD of Berber music and I am crazy about it. A sort of mix between Berber music and rock. It's fantastic, very powerful. I do have Berber tattoos on my hand and the first Jewish people were Berber, therefor it inspires me a lot. Some of my ancestors must have been Berber.

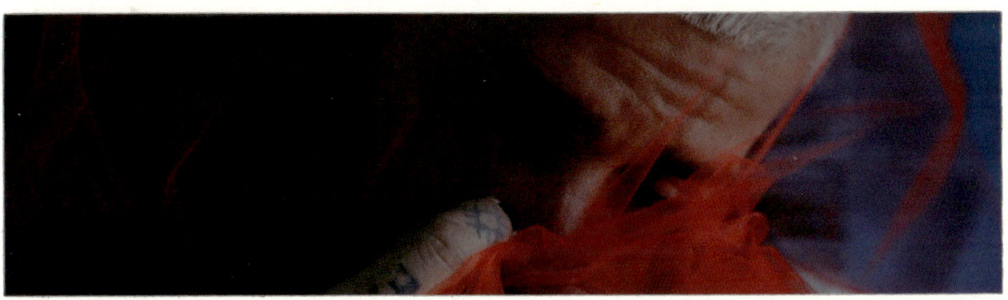

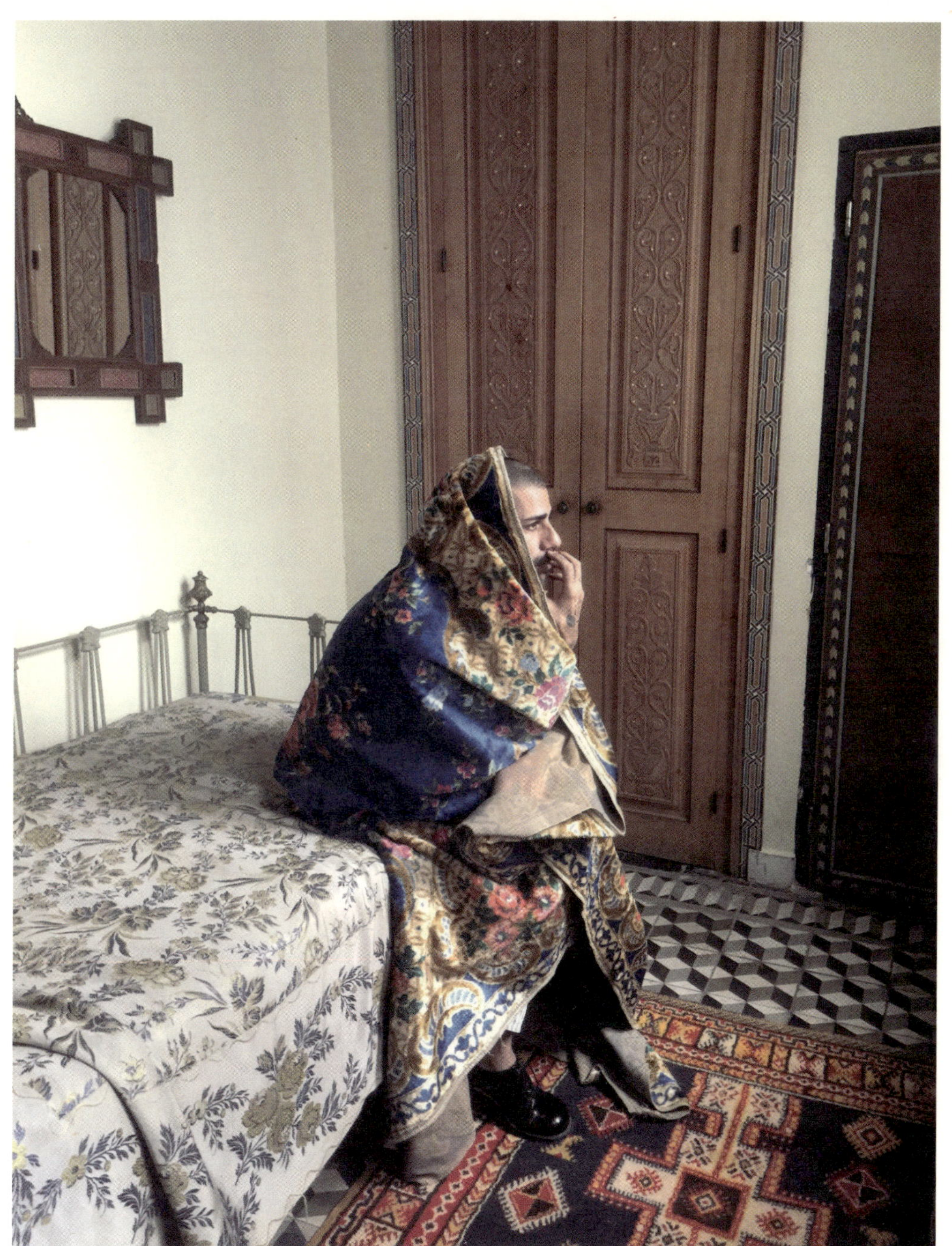

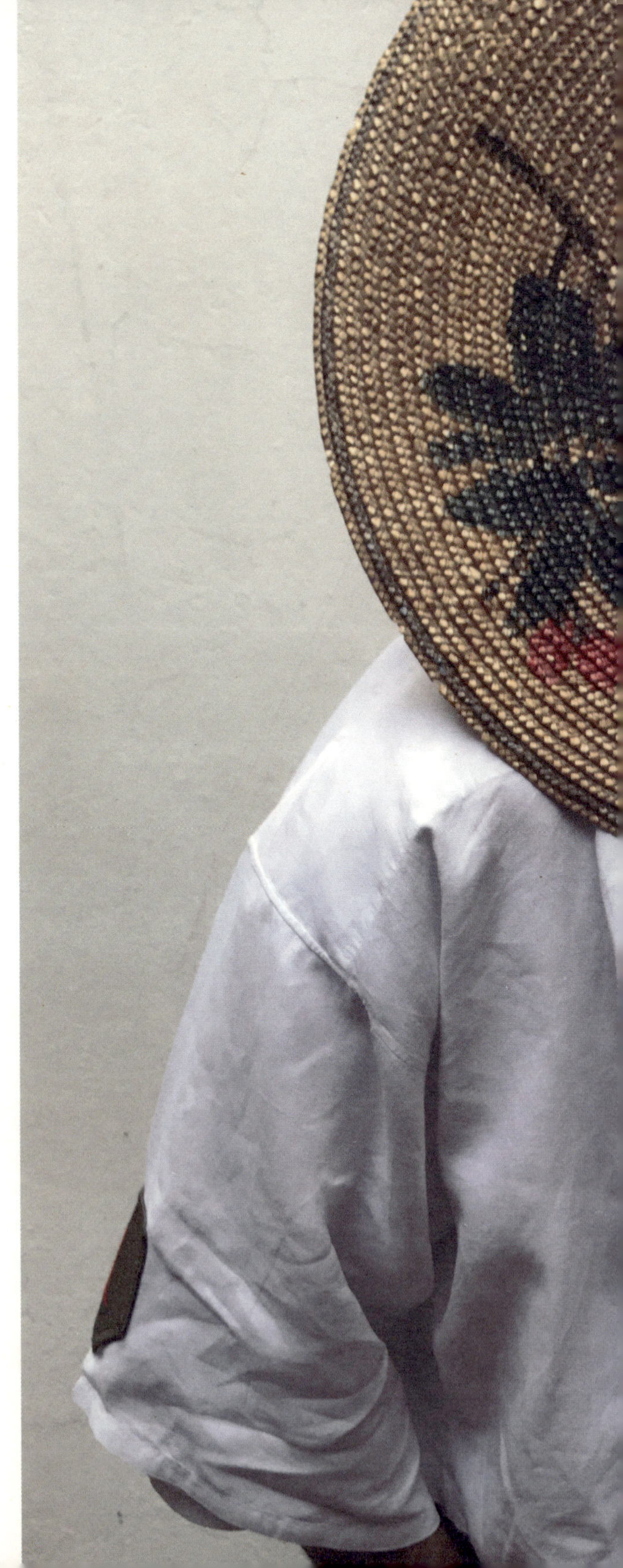

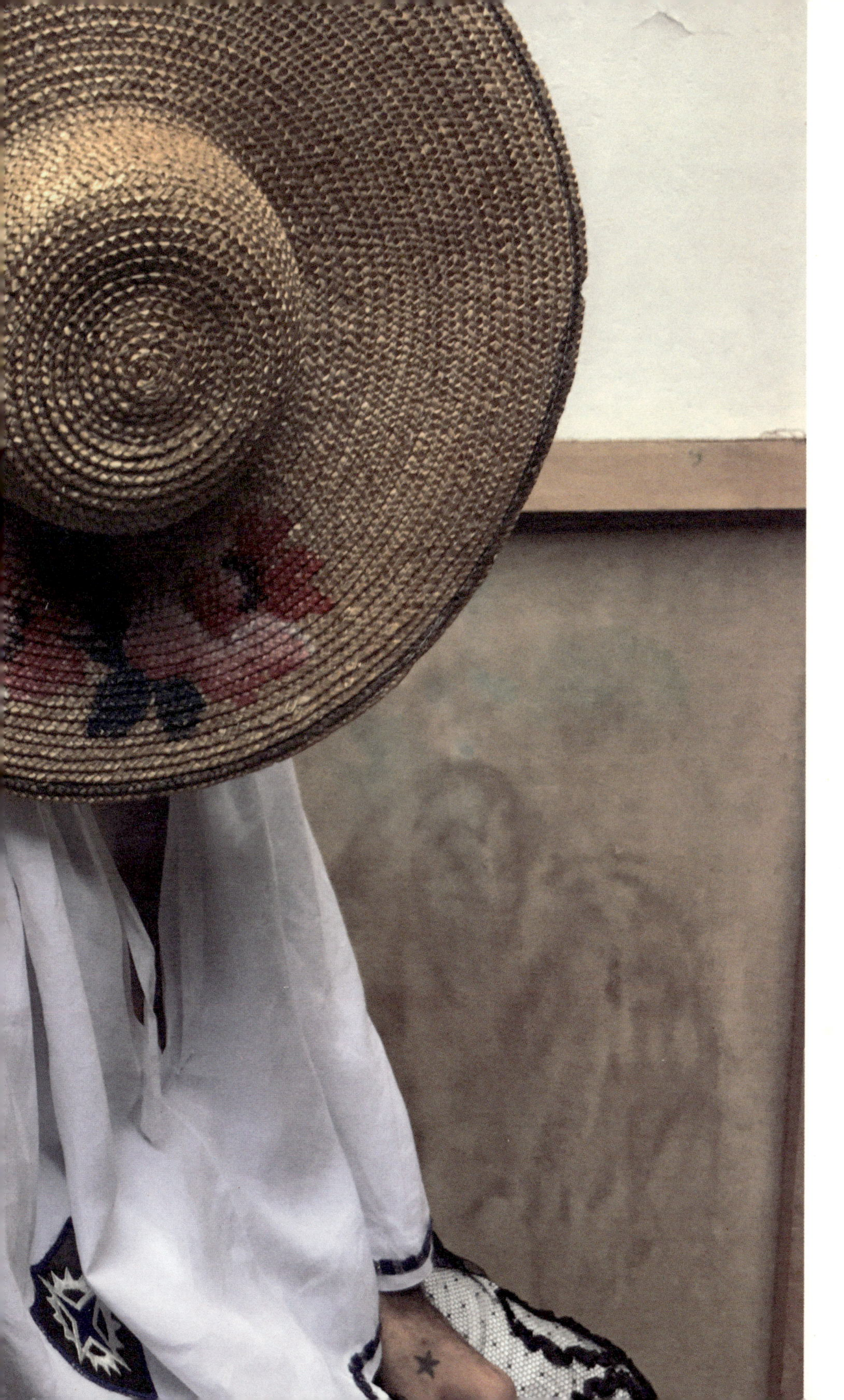

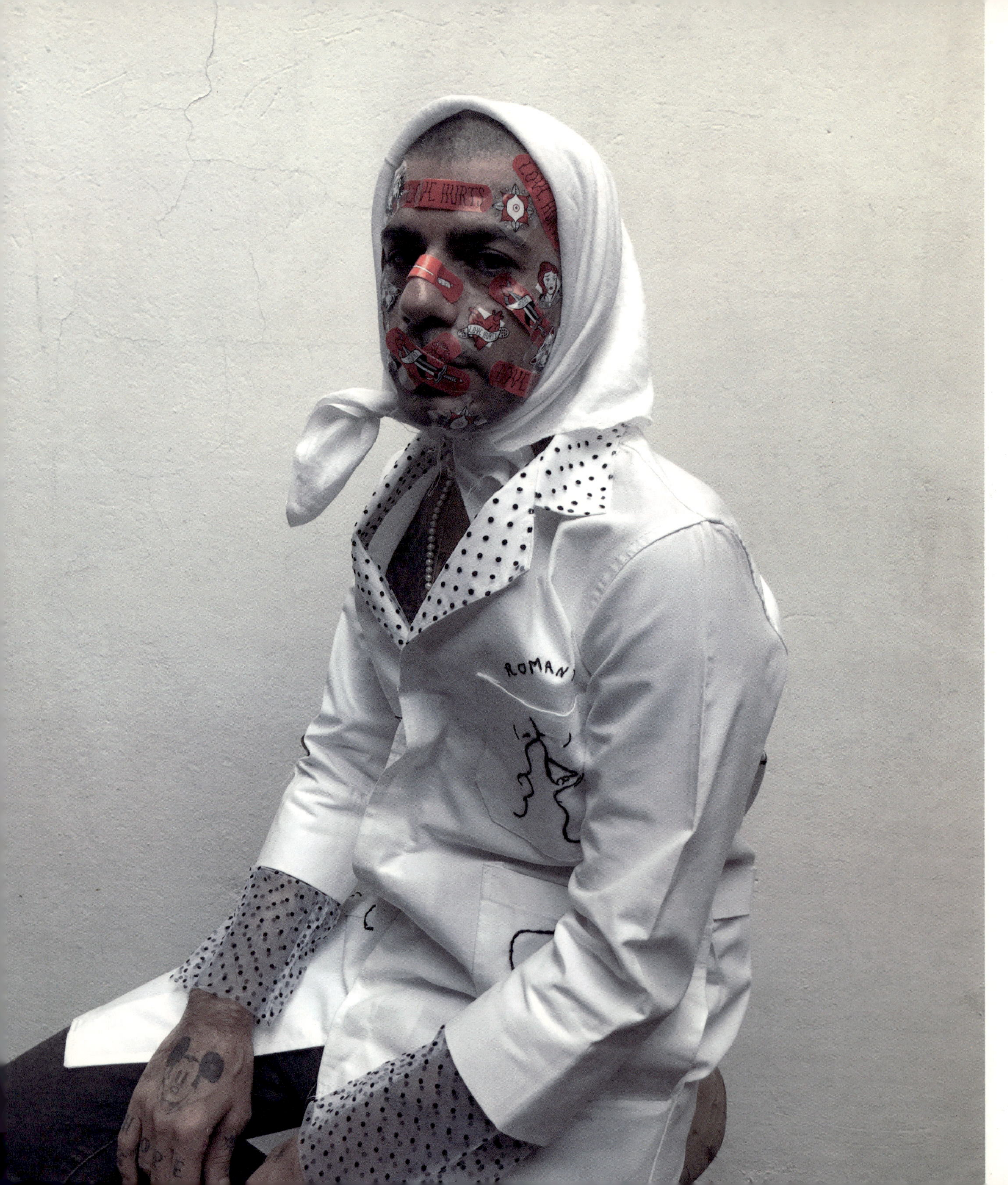
LOVE HURTS
LOVE HURTS

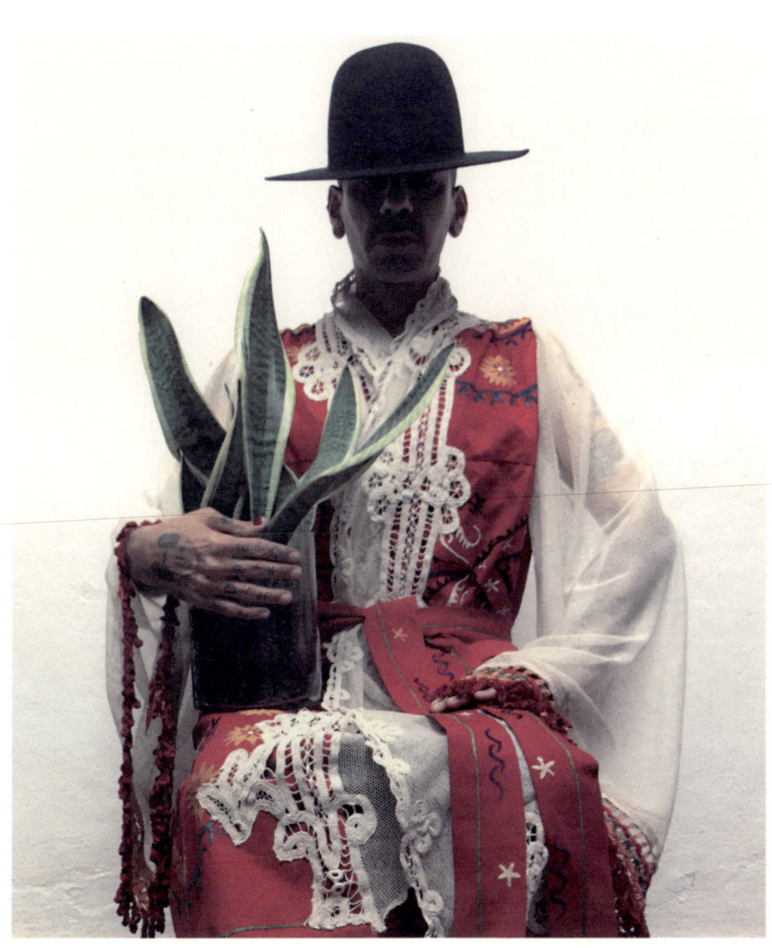

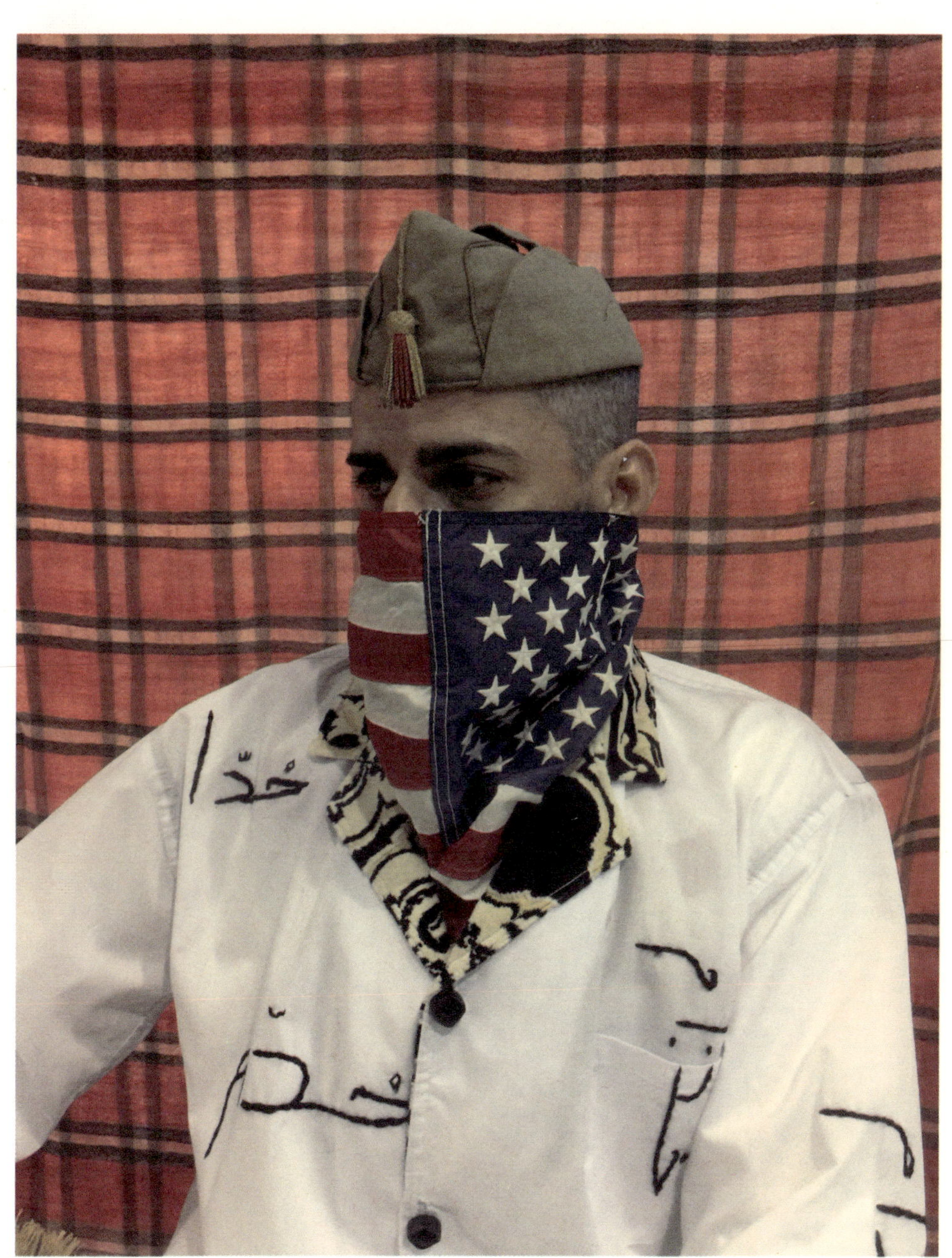

Rinat Aboulafia

Some designers don't like when people tell them their design has an ethnic or folkloric style. Do you get that too and does it disturb you?

So, you can't really define or give a name to your style?

OK. That is a nice name.

Which means that you can't be really stuck. You are always between ups and downs.

Your work contains obsession and discipline. I have often been curious of your notebook filled up with your beautiful handwriting. A lot of things are going on in your work, especially through your obsessive layering.

To take a picture every day, demands discipline. What wakes you up in the morning?

To whom?

Yes, I know.

What do you love about yourself?

Let's be a little more specific. Go from head to toe.

Yes, I think it's the most important love. When you love yourself, you can start loving the others.

Artsi Ifrach

With whatever I do, or am, or dress up with, if I had to consider what people like or not, I wouldn't be able to do any of the things I do, so I don't even consider it as something that can influence my work. When I work I come from such a free place. I don't think about the likes and dislikes it might take. I deliver something very personal and hopefully it becomes for the others too. But it does not have to do with liking it or not, otherwise I empower what blocks creativity nowadays.

There is a name for my style. It's Artsi.

If you write it in English, it means art. So, I call my mother every Friday and thank her for giving me this name. In Hebrew is very interesting because the meaning of Artsi Ifrach means ups and downs at the same time. It's my feminine side.

Yes, it also means happiness in Arabic.

Discipline means a lot to me. As Napoleon said: "There is a very fine line between the sublime and the ridicule". And this fine line is easy to reach, without discipline and order I would always end up to the ridicule. I use my intuition to know when I get there. I always try to do better, the more I evolve with my work, the more it's *raffiné*.

Love.

To myself, and to my work. To what I do. I love myself very much.

It's very important, because I think it's the only way I can give it back.

Everything.

I love the person that I'm becoming. I love the person that makes mistakes, and try to fix them. I love that I'm disciplined, that I can take all this love and put it in what I love the most. Without love, I couldn't do it. I love the freedom that I have, the spirit that I put in things. Everybody should love themselves first. It's some advice.

The research is not outside, but inside and that's what I'm constantly doing. It's much more comfortable.

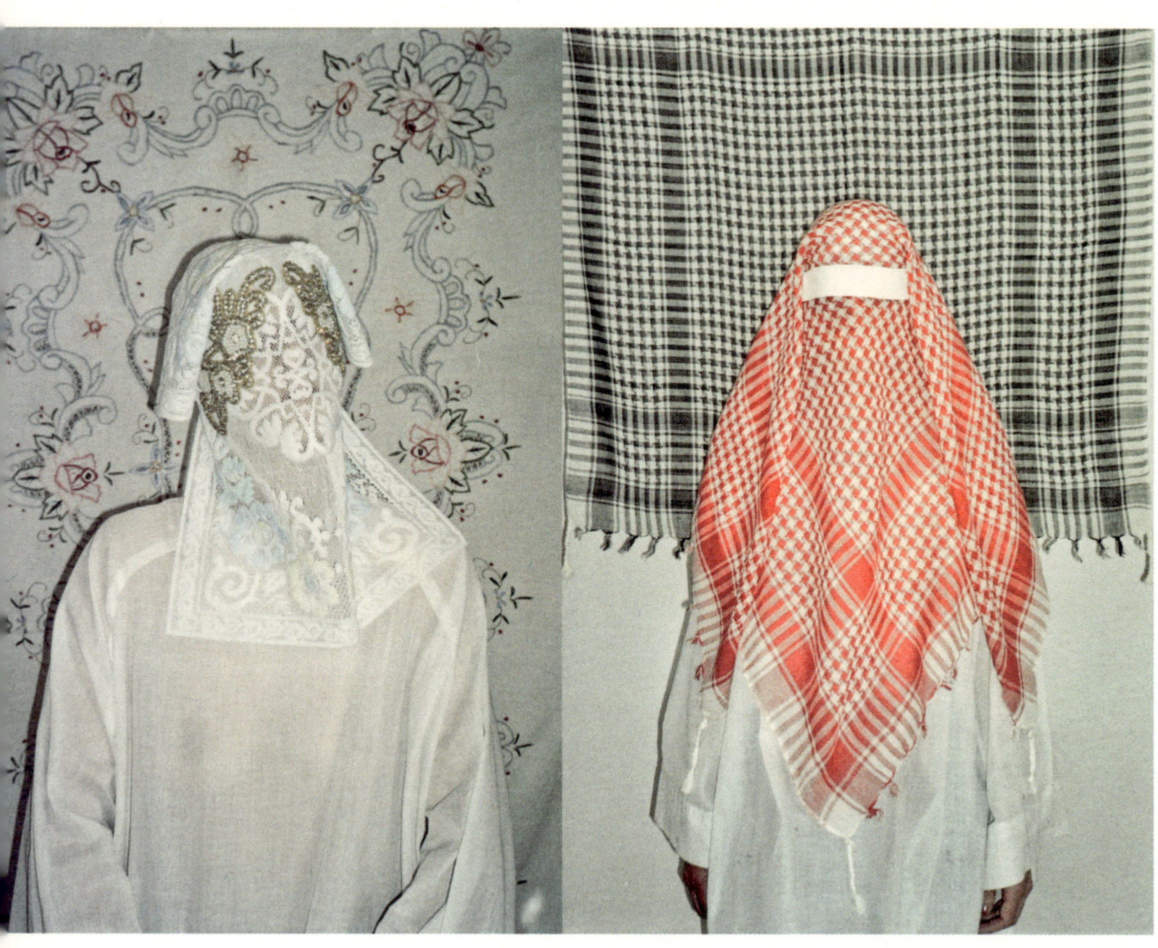

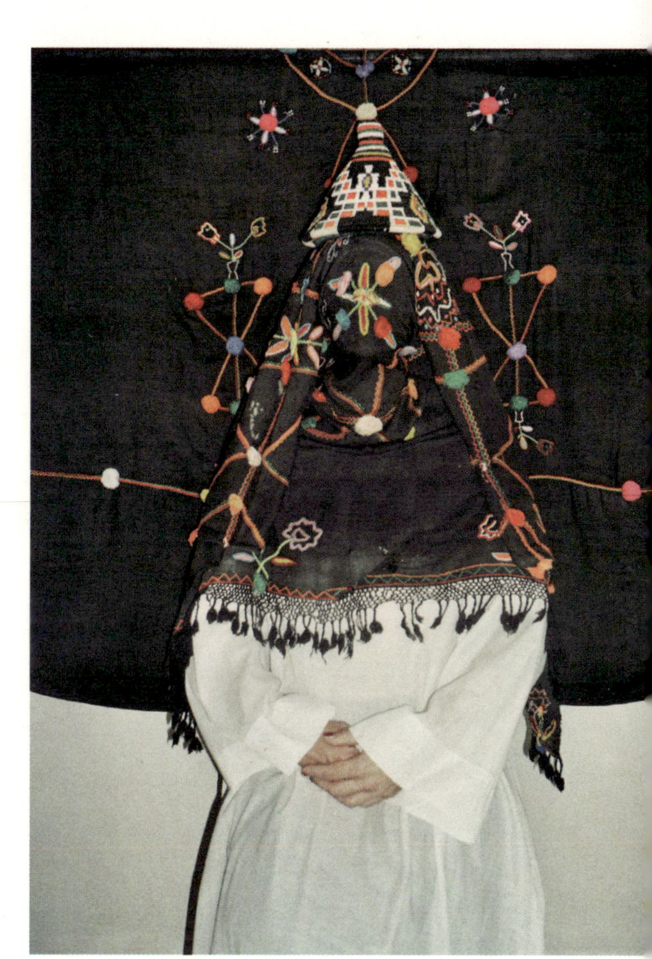

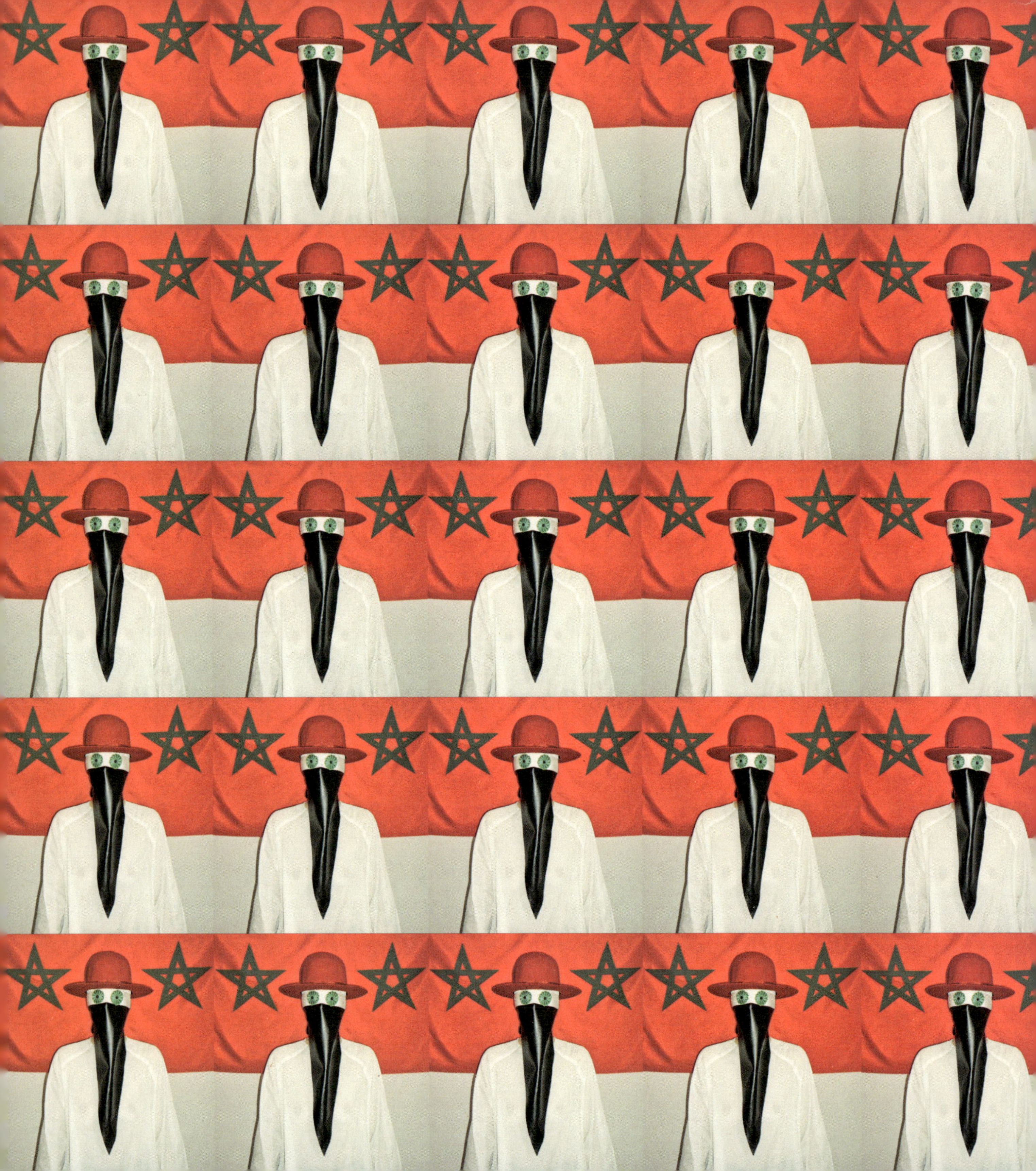

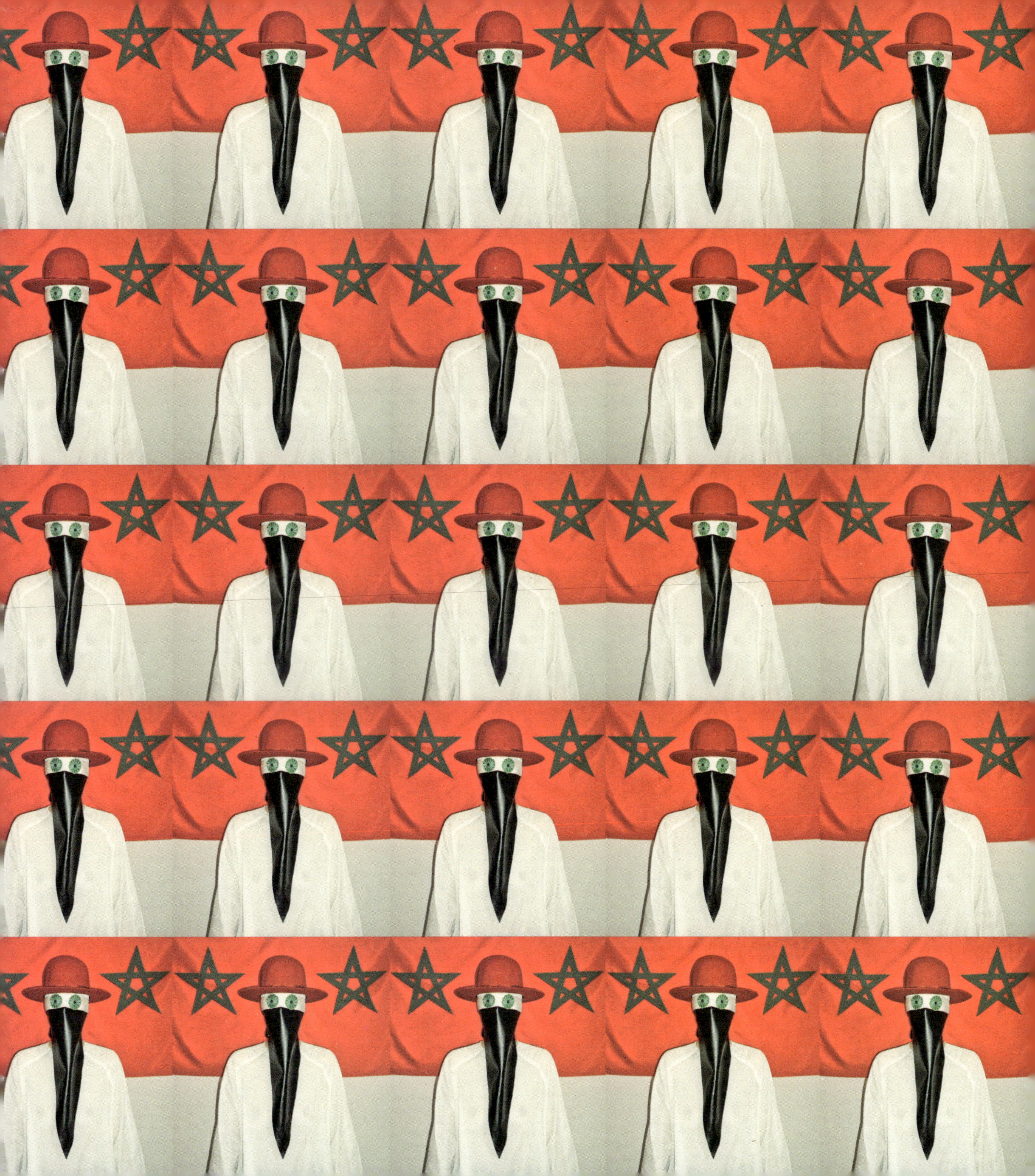

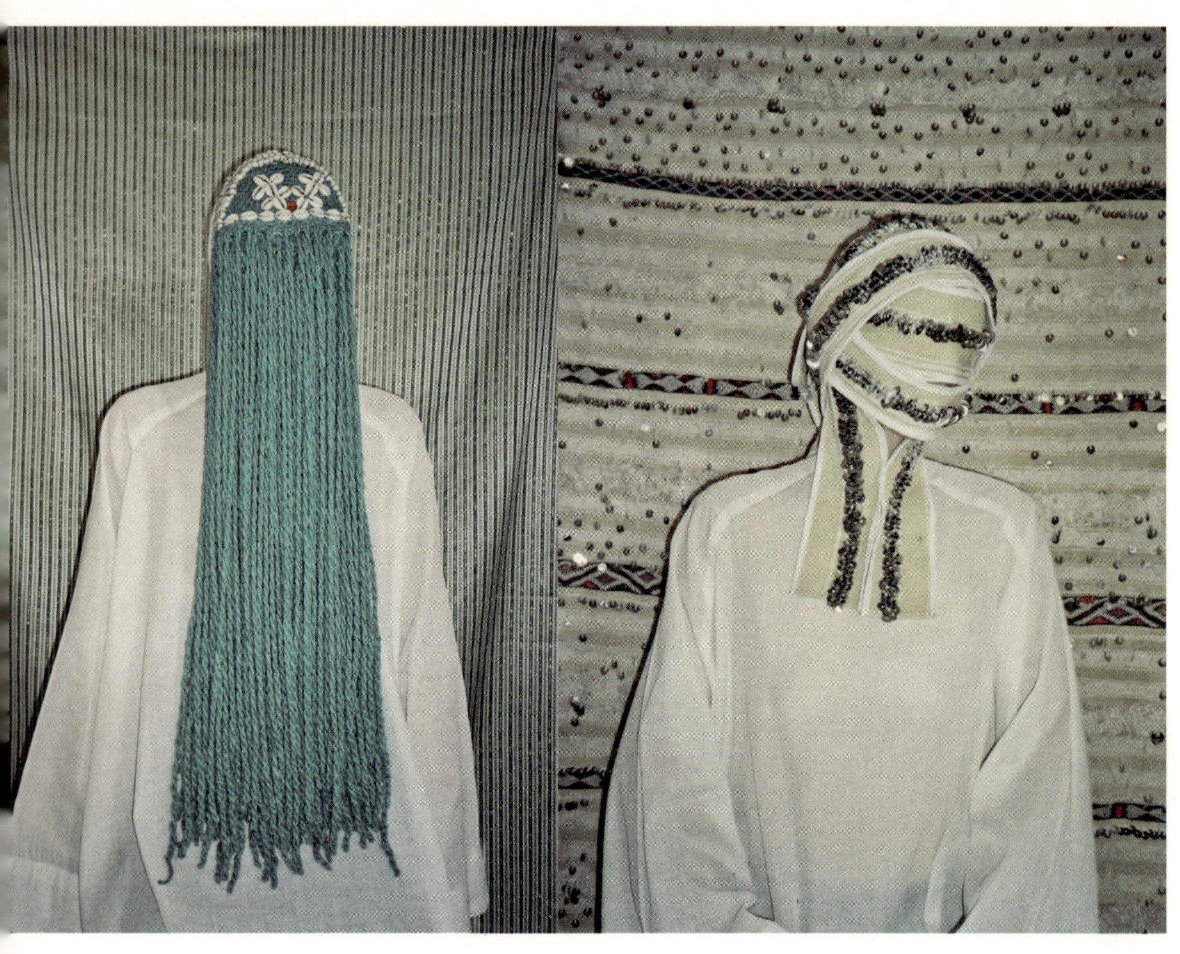

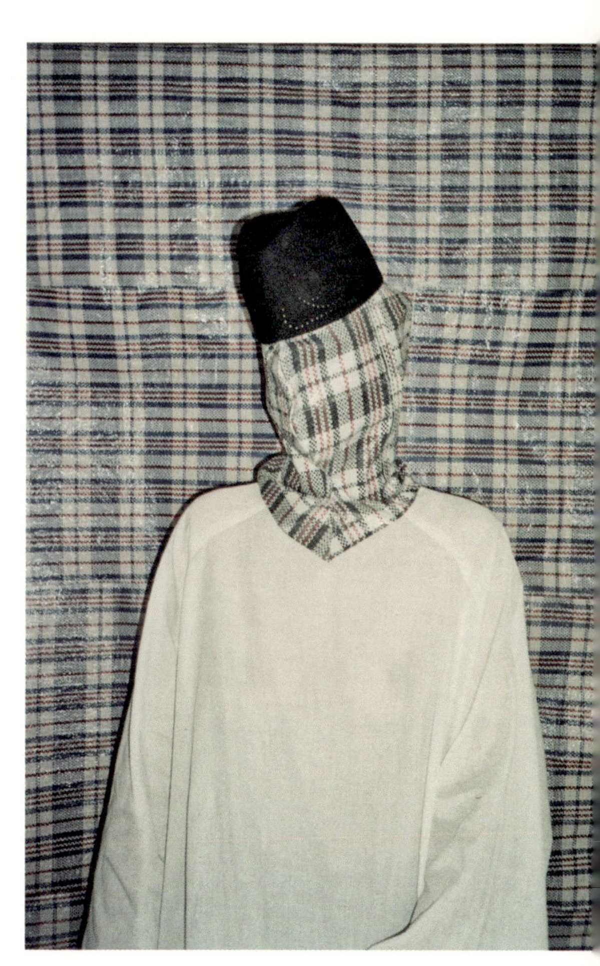

Rinat Aboulafia

What is fashion for you?

Can you say more about the core?

Is there anybody in the fashion world who is doing the right thing?

Is there someone you look up to?

You don't want to insult anyone?

So, if you don't want to talk about others, let's go back to you. Do you feel any different designing for men as opposed to designing for women? "Prince Charming" is the name of your last collection. You said it's a collection for men that women would like to wear.

You are very colorful. What do you think about the black color?

I'm trying to understand... In your view, there is no difference between designing for men and designing for women?

You are very colorful. What do you think about the black color?

Artsi Ifrach

I like taking risks. Taking risks provokes something new. It does not have to be beautiful, but it has to be different. I'm not trying to be anybody but myself, so I'm very conscious of what I do and I try to be disciplined about it. To do what I do is very specific and it reaches a niche. It's an essence, like a perfume. I try to find the essence that creates the perfume, the core of everything. To me, what I do is the core of fashion and from there we can open to other things.

I think there is a lot of creativity in our days, but I don't think we see that kind of creativity because we are busier with following the mass people, we try to pack everything in a way that will be easier for people to like it. I try to be individual and create something that is private for me but might touch some other people. I don't think about finance, how big it will be, how many people will buy it. It does not influence me in any way.

There are a lot of creators doing the right thing. I have a lot of respect for people who wake up in the morning and wonder what they will create next, that is new or different.

I look up to many.

No, it's not about insulting. The biggest problem in fashion is that everyone is trying to be better than the other. The solution is that no one has to be better, but everyone has to be different. I was influenced by many.

I create pieces that can go to women, men, anyone. A piece goes to a point where it does not have a gender. I don't design sexy. That part matters for the sales aspect of fashion, rather than fashion itself. Of course, someone can look very sexy, but we are talking about dressing up and not being naked. We are dressing up, not dressing down. When you are dressing up, you are wearing garments. I'm more interested in the silhouettes, the colour, the movements. I think we all are actors. We dress up tying to define, characterise ourselves, sending a message of who we are. There is no necessity of gender.

Not anymore, no.

The painter's canvas is white, black has become the canvas of fashion. I don't deal so much with black, as I don't feel challenged by this color. You cannot go wrong with black.

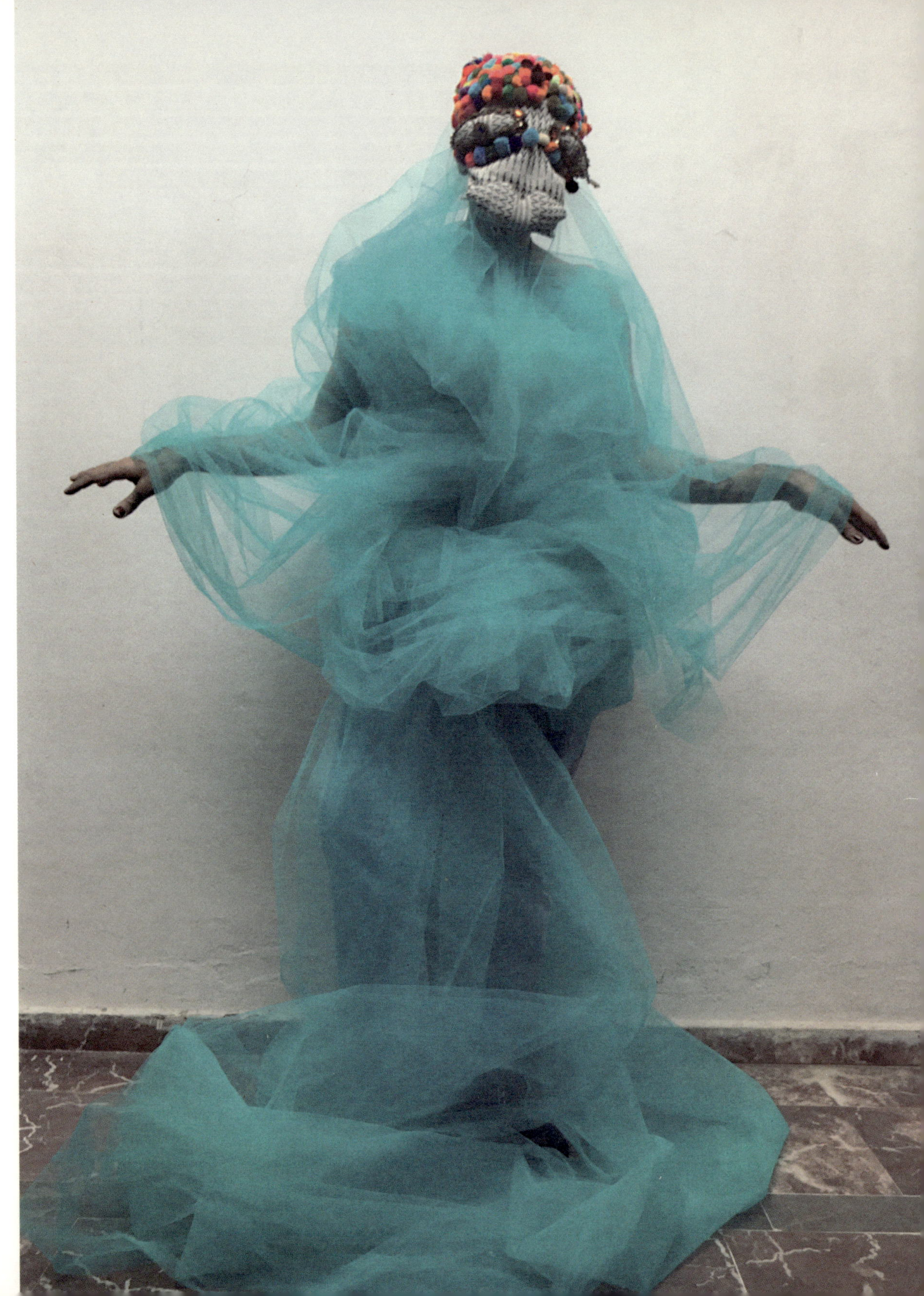

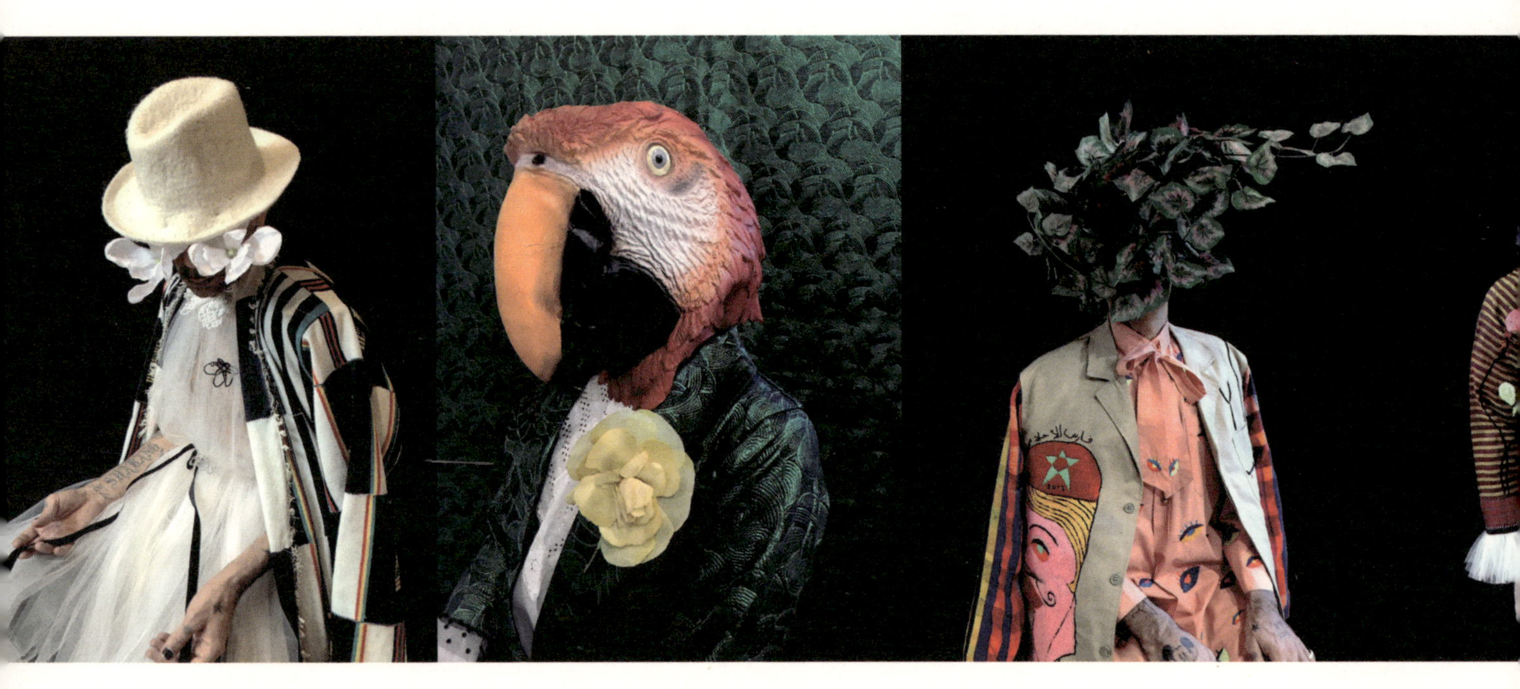

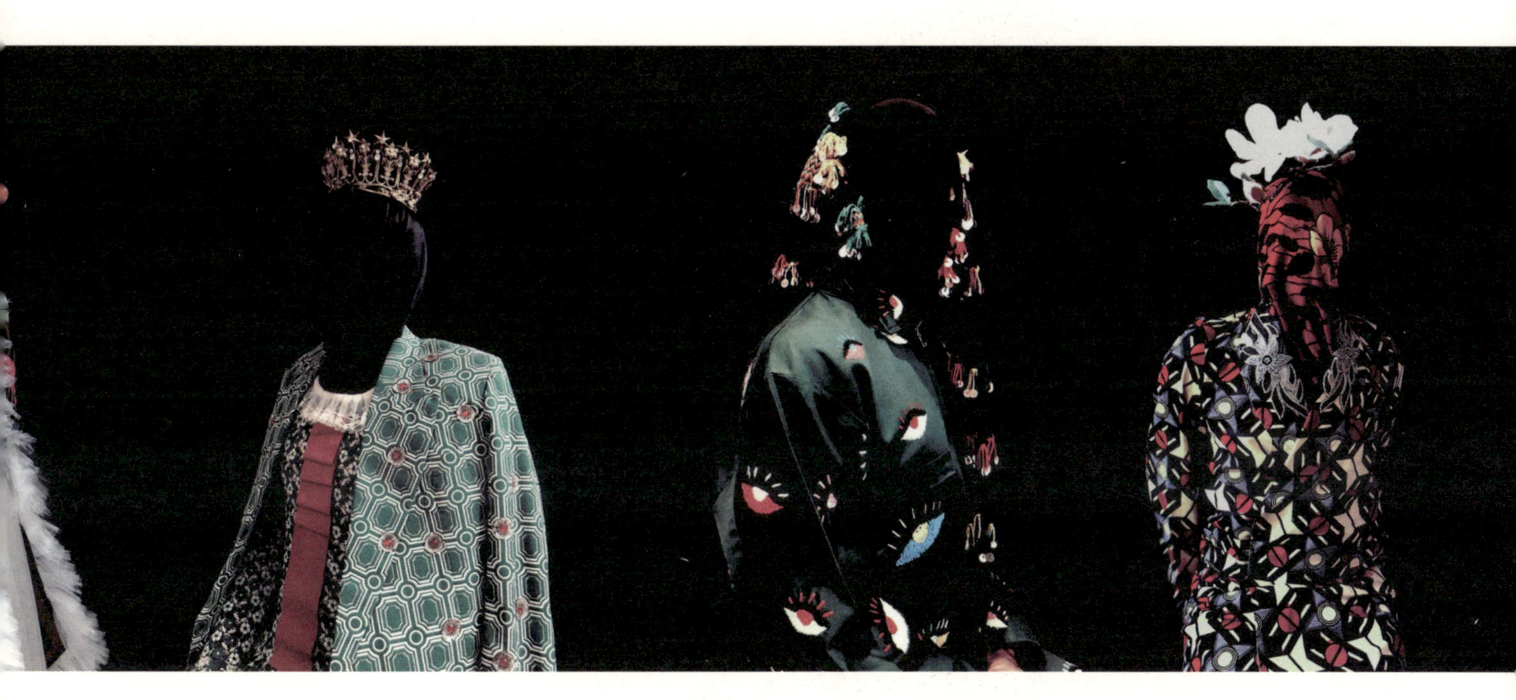

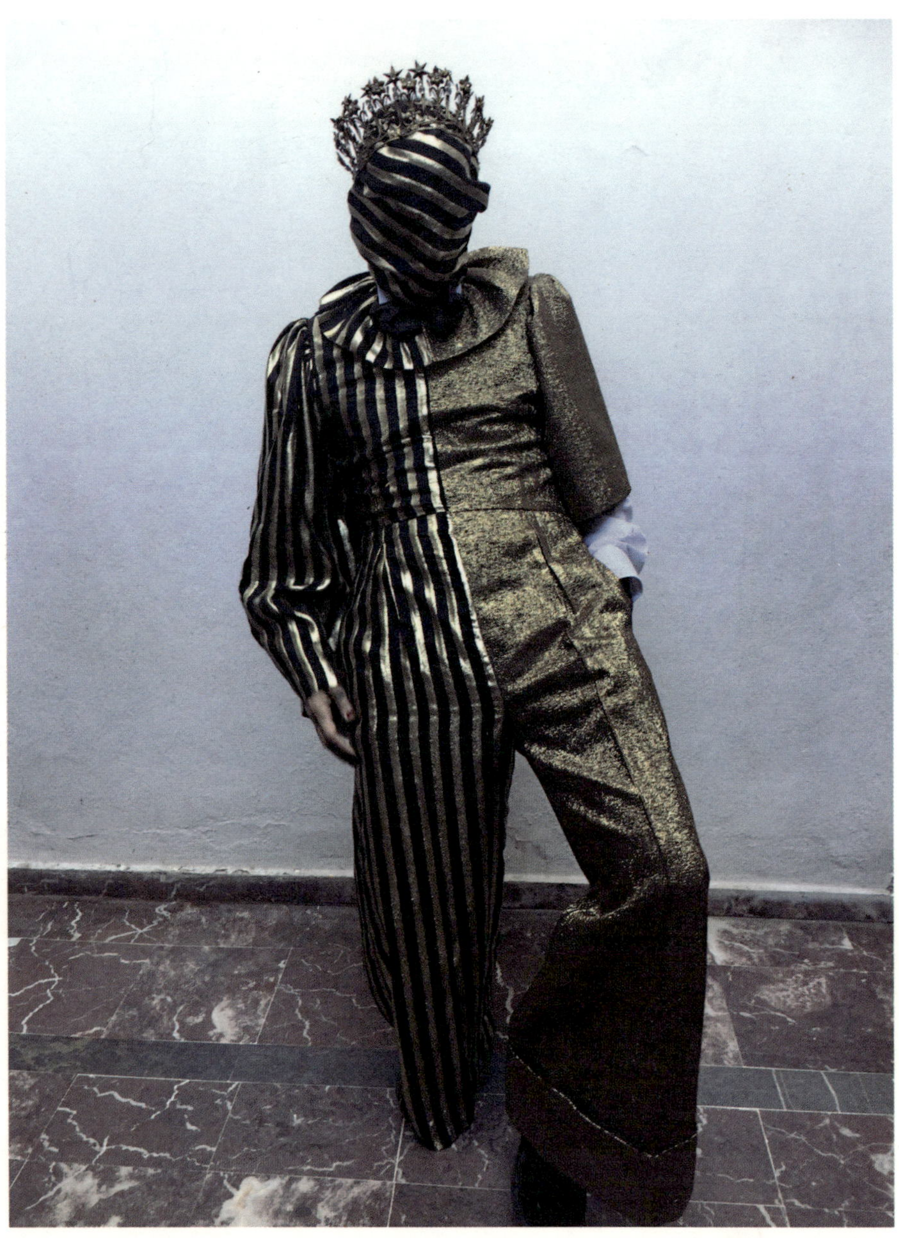

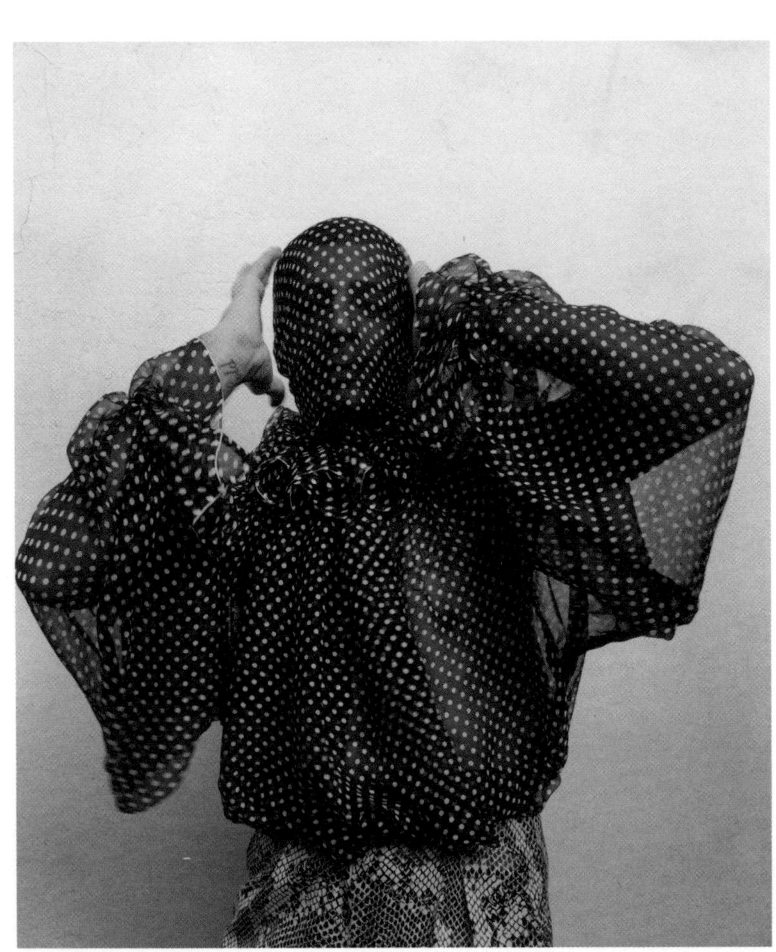

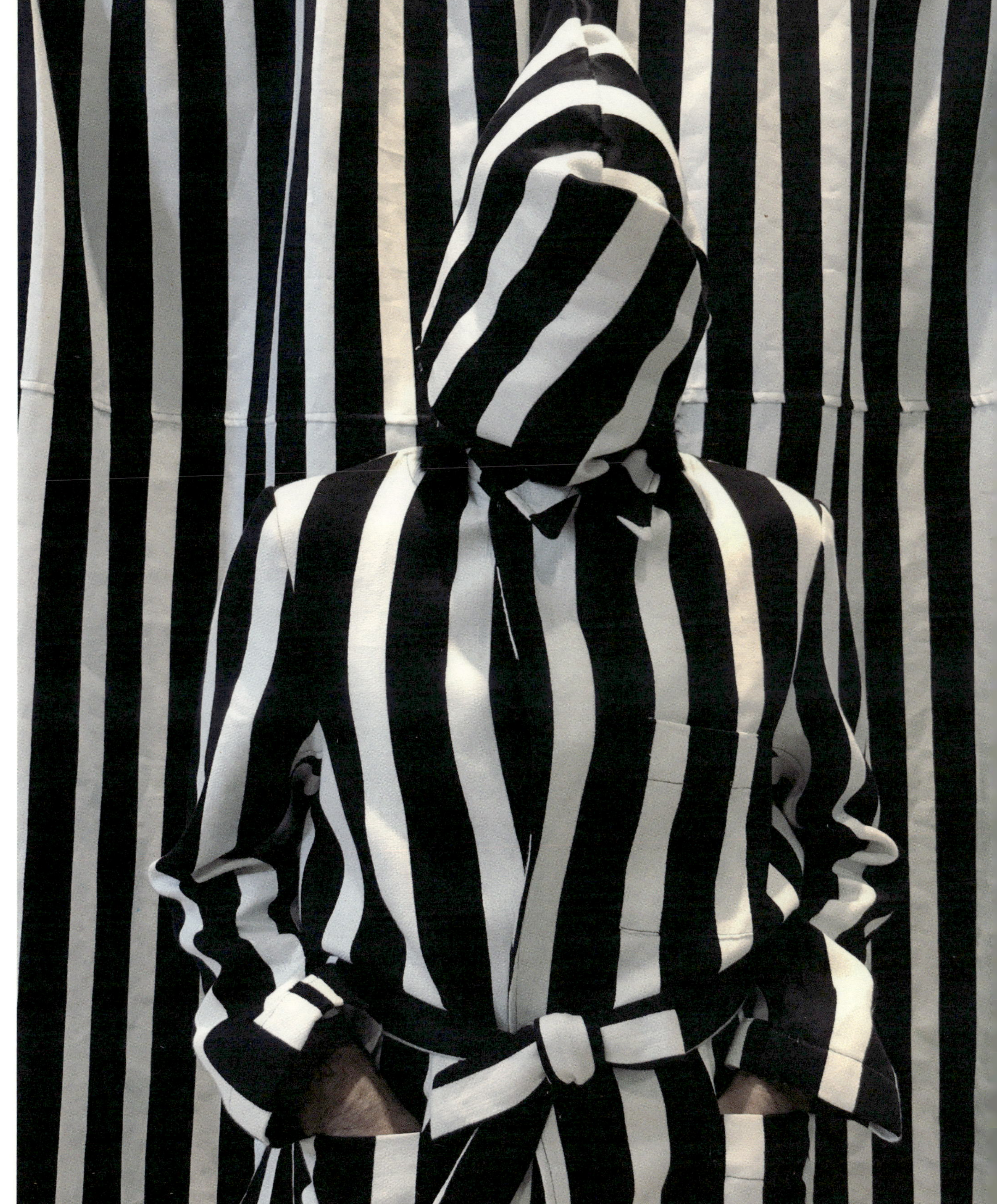

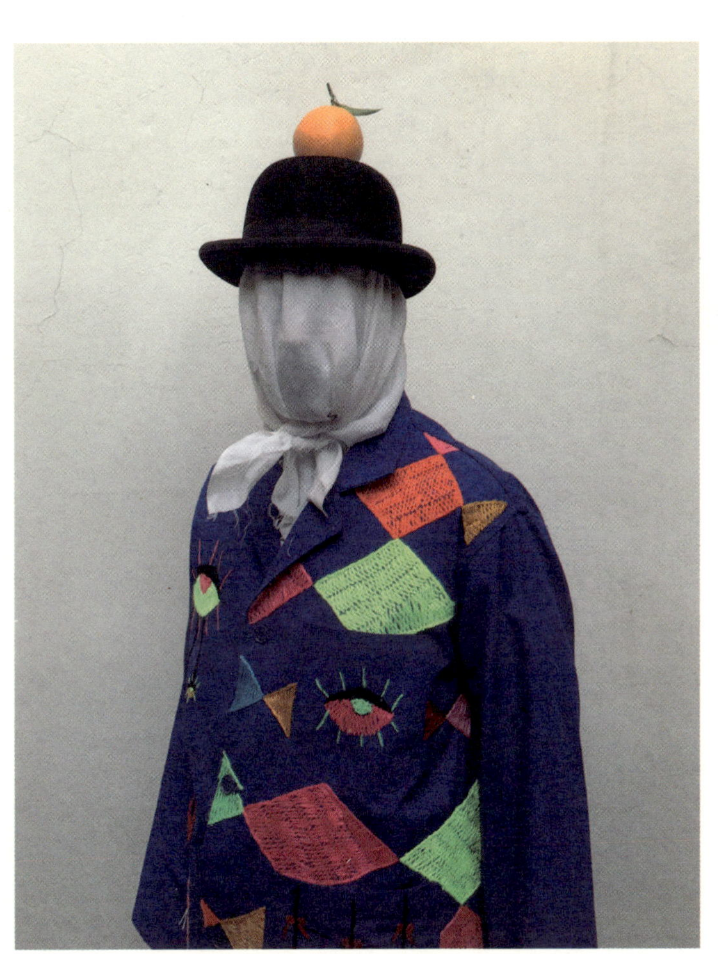

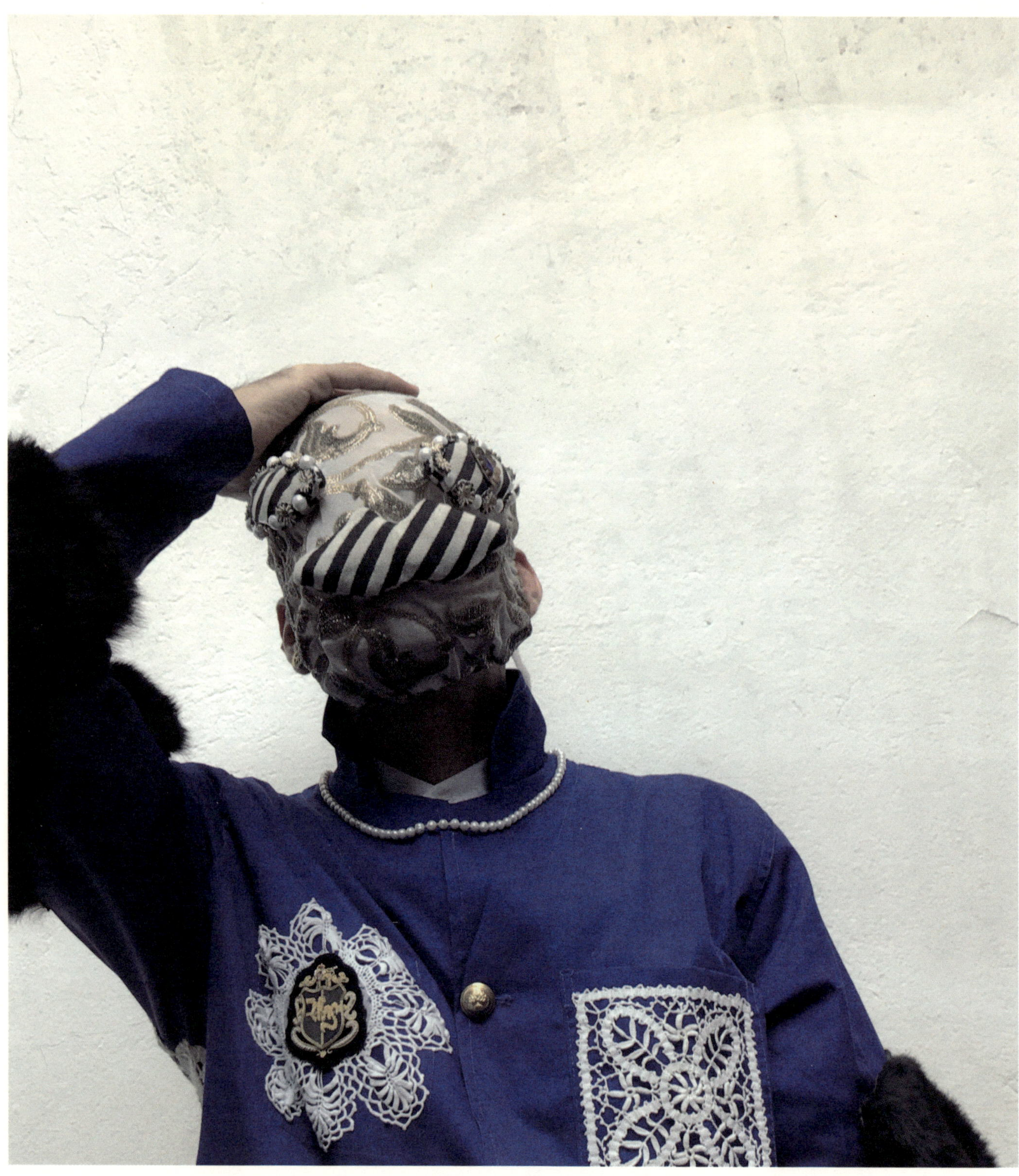

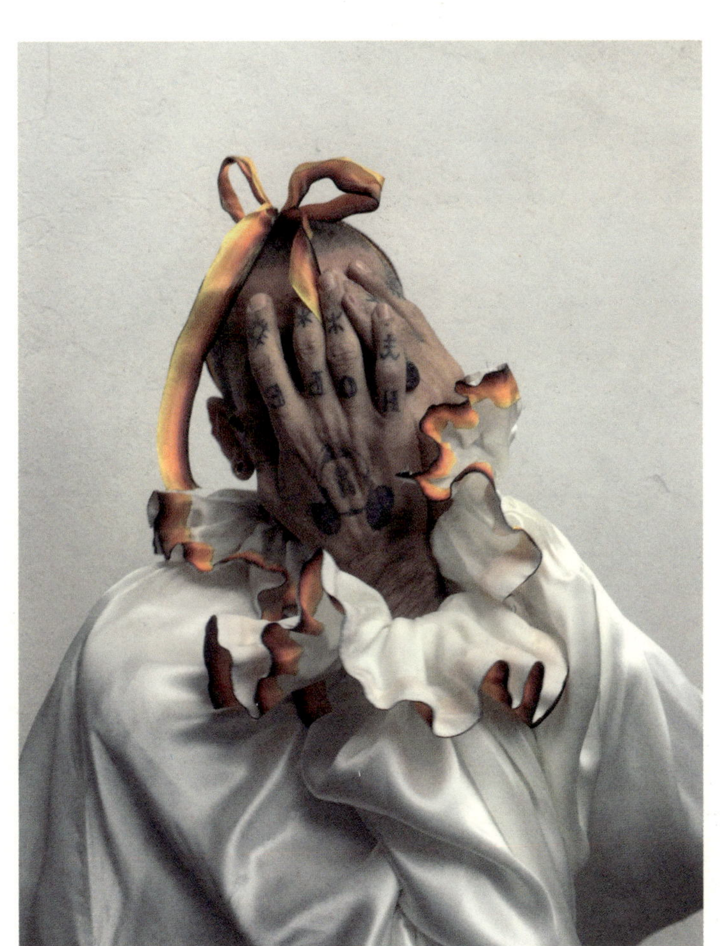

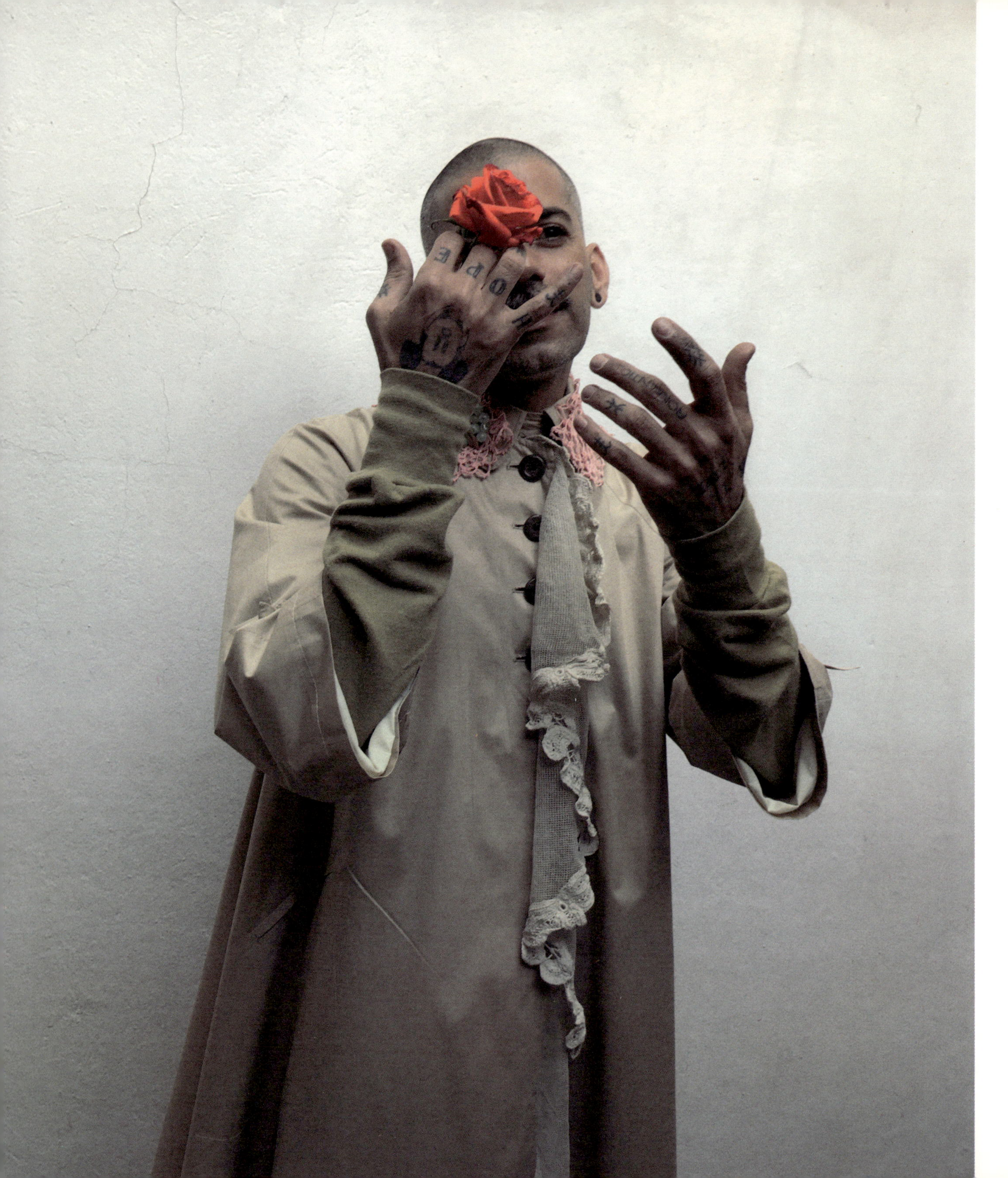
HOPE

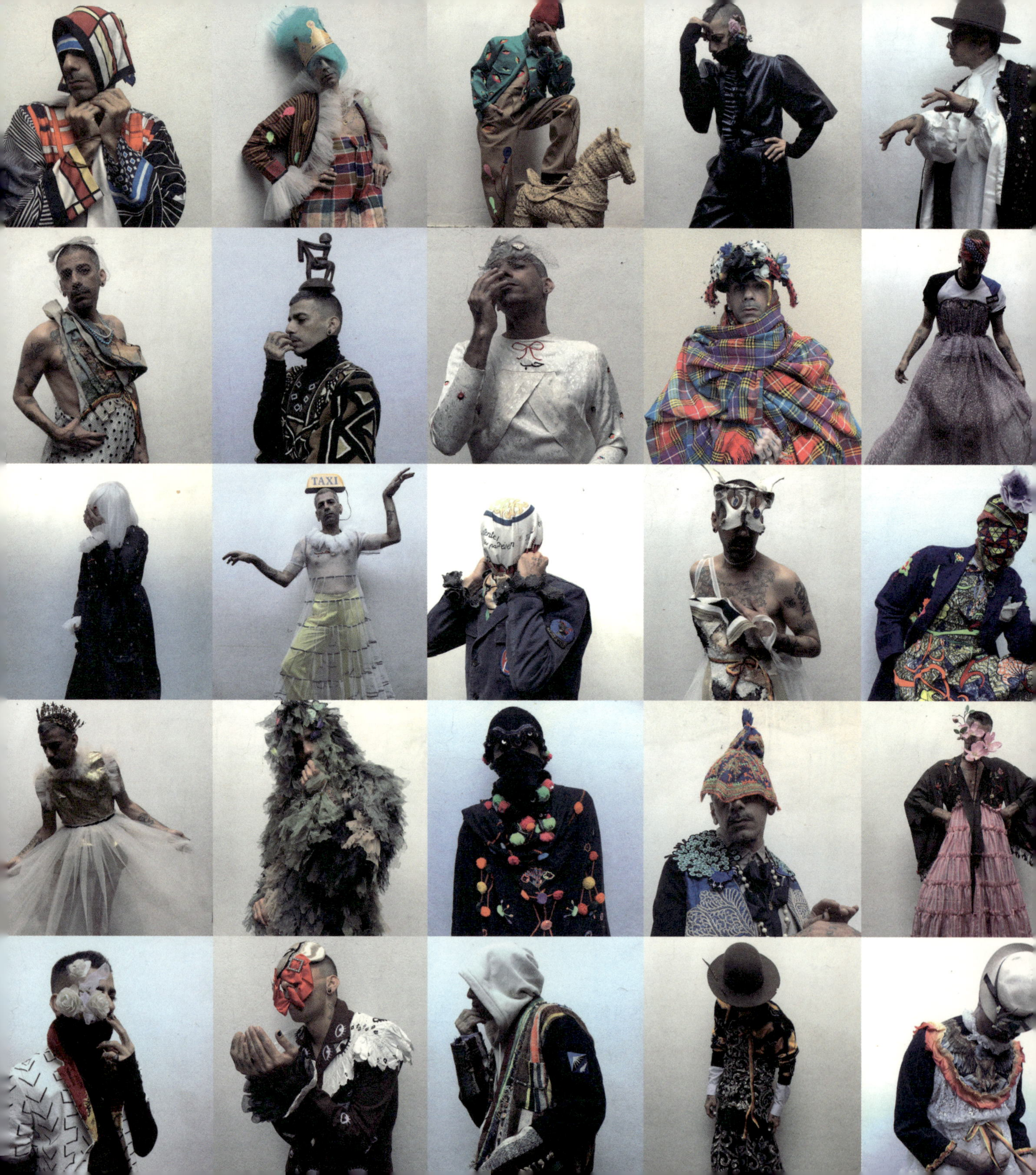
حب
TAXI

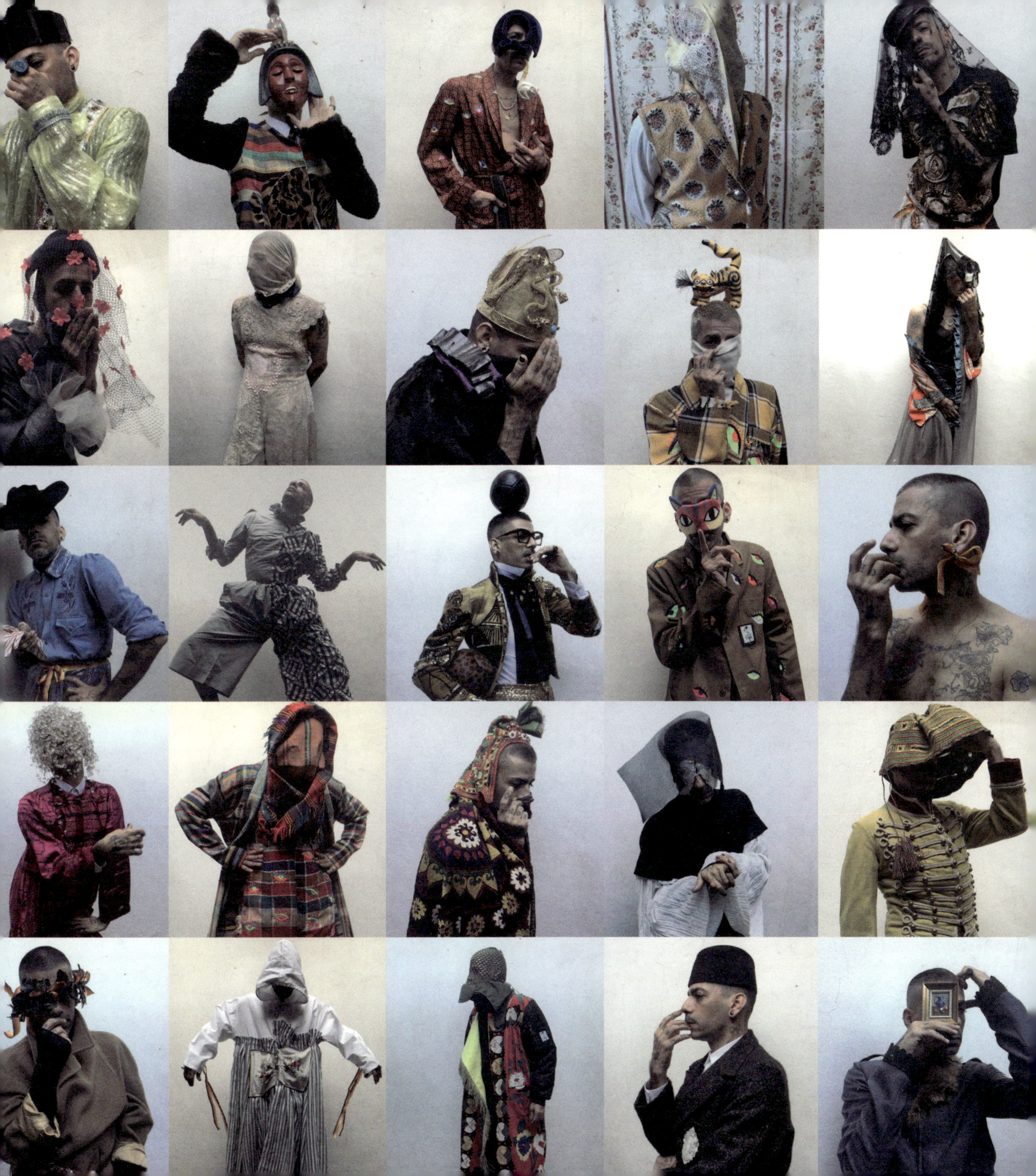

Rinat Aboulafia

Every day you post a new picture on Instagram. You call it "Picture of the day". This book is all about this body of work that you have been doing for a year now. I look at the details and I recognise the skills of a stylist and a designer. What is the process behind it? Do you think about it beforehand?

You make one piece a day?

Do you think your mask is the masculine answer to the vale that Muslim women wear?

Go on with the process of making "Picture of the day".

And who takes the pictures?

We see different backgrounds.

And you do this every day.

You are a passionate storyteller.

So, the whole Instagram posting is actually about you creating a diary.

Artsi Ifrach

I started as a stylist but I quickly felt I couldn't find enough space for what my imagination was telling me to do. So I told myself I had to create something. Therefore I started with the "Picture of the day" and the whole process behind it. First of all, I create a piece I would like to have. So, I start as a designer, but I don't make a collection as I used to do in the past. I make only on-of-a-kind pieces.

One piece, every day. When it's ready, I take a picture and through the image I try to tell a story. The inspiration comes at any time. I'm very intuitive and I collect a lot of things. As a stylist, I used to have a lot of props, I'm crazy about masks, as you can see.

I never thought about that, in the subconscious, maybe. I do think that there is something interesting about wearing a mask. There again you can be anything you want without revealing yourself.

I will give you an example. One of my favorite pictures is the man wearing black-and-white pajamas with a yellow taxi sign as a hat. Whenever a Jew sees a combination of black, white and yellow he immediately thinks of the Holocaust. While I was creating the suit, black and white with a vintage fur collar I found at the flea market, a strong question came to me. I wondered why black and white stripes and the yellow colour should always evoke the memory of the Holocaust. So I went to a shop that sells everything for cars, and I bought the yellow taxi sign. I decided to use it for the picture. The point was to reference the Holocaust but also to fix the memory. So now when I think about this image, I don't think about a Jew with black-and-white pyjamas and a yellow star, I think about a guy wearing a funny suit and wearing the taxi sign on his head. Somehow, this is my process.

Bushra, she is my right hand. She has been working for me for many years now. She takes a lot of pictures and by phone. I then choose one and edit it.

I always build the whole set.

Yes, every day. It's like people going to the gym or having breakfast. Again, it's called discipline. It's like an exercise for your creativity.

I tell stories through pictures, through my pieces. At the end of the day, I sell all those pieces. Most of the pieces you can see in the pictures are already gone, they were sold to clients. The only thing left is the picture.

It's a diary. And I hope that I can do it for many years to come. Hopefully, I will be lucky enough.

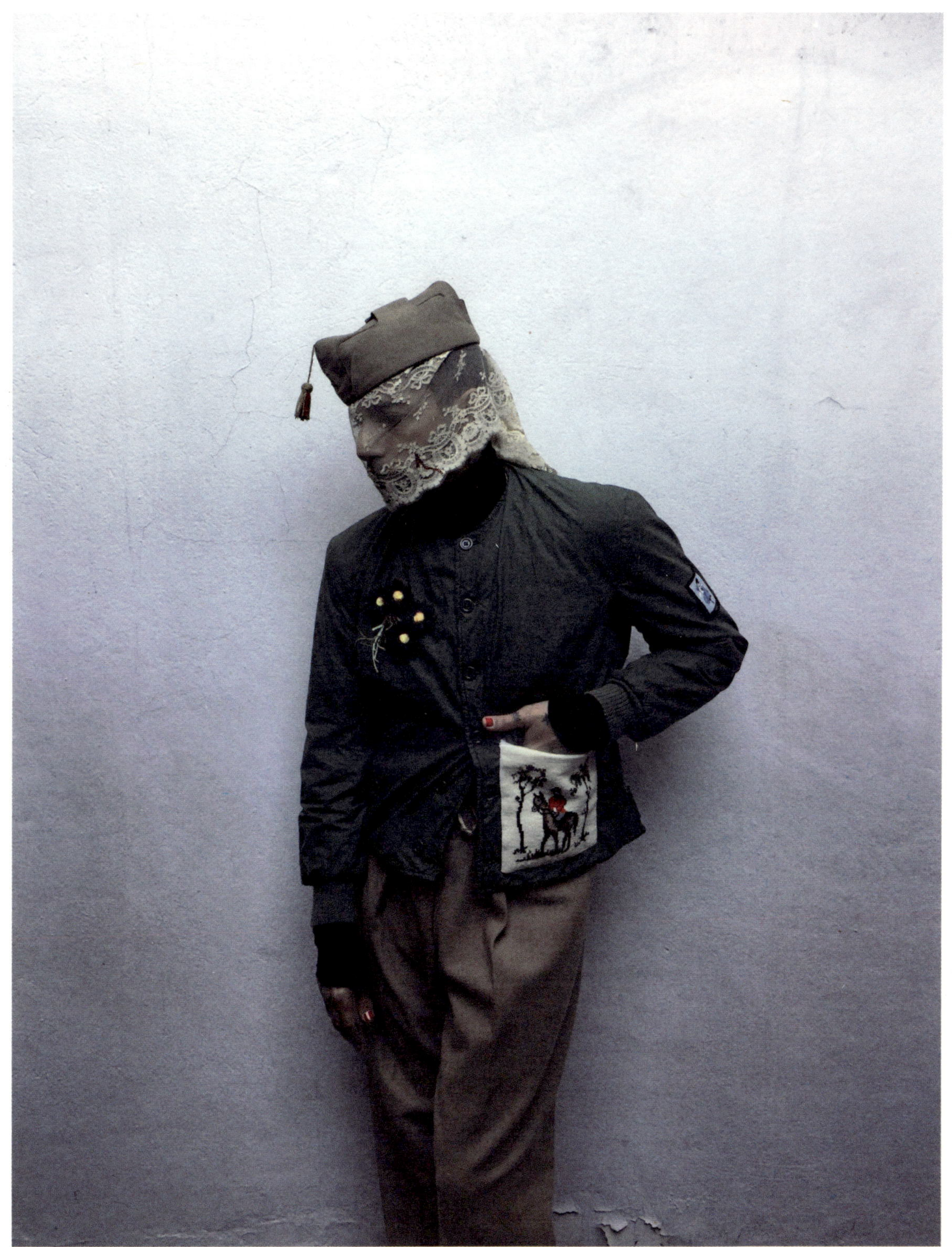

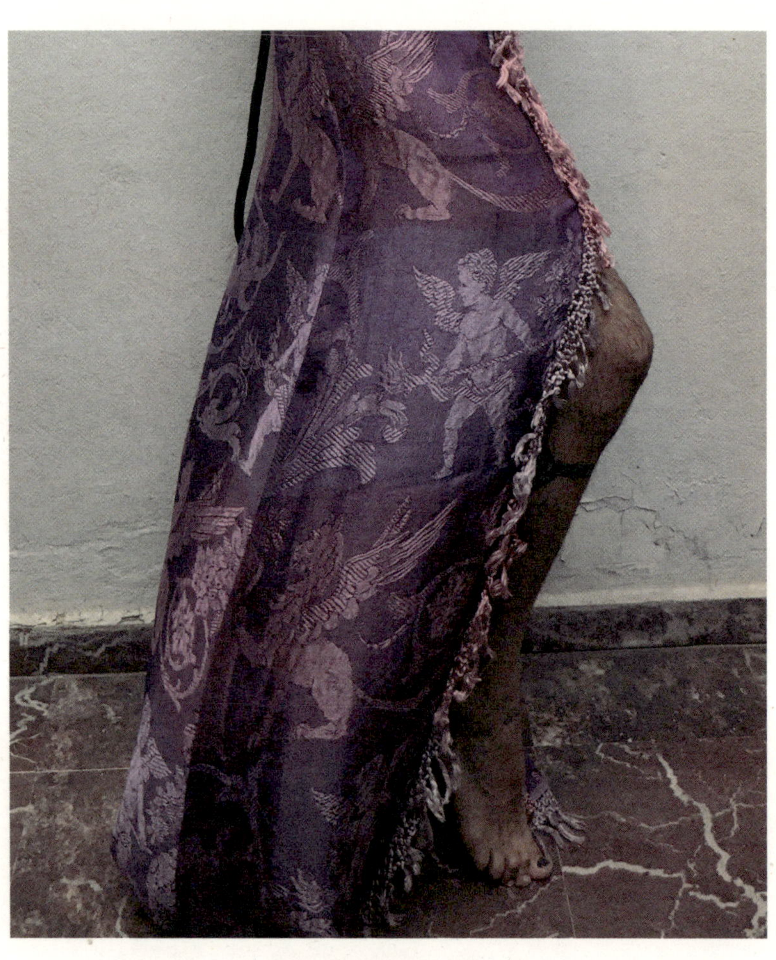

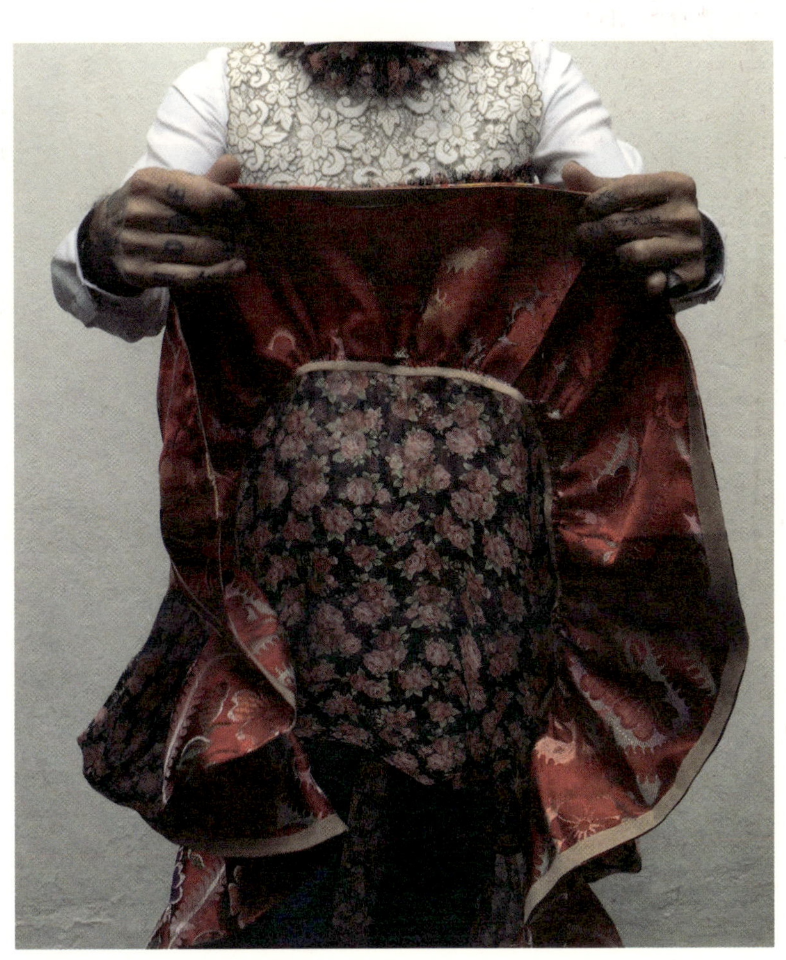

Rinat Aboulafia

Do you ever fear that you might lose your touch?

Don't you ever hesitate?

So you are a political person but sometimes you choose not to share it.

I wanted to ask you about the symbol of the eyes. You often use it on your garments. What are they looking for?

You also apply words on your garments. What words do you use and why are all of them in Arabic?

Do I have to be a diva to wear your pieces?

It seems to me that in the "Pictures of the day", you are really telling people that they should be dressed as they want.

What is the future of everything?

Artsi Ifrach

Everybody is afraid. I'm afraid of many things, but I don't feel fear in my work. It's the only place where I feel safe. I'm not afraid of my creativity neither of the way I'm dressed and act. Today, lots of people can't exercise this kind of freedom so I question it every day.

No. Sometimes I take pictures that are too political, which I deal a lot with. I keep them for myself. But I don't hesitate when I take them.

Of course, like everybody, I have an opinion.

In the Arab world, the eye is a symbol of protection from "The evil eye", which is not my case. To me, it symbolises the only tool through which you can actually see things. Without eyes, you cannot see beauty. Of course, we can imagine it.

I mainly write Prince Charming, freedom, love, hope and I use the Arabic language because it's a beautiful one. It's wonderful to see it translated into embroideries. Language is important, but the way you write it's even more important.

Nobody has to be a diva. I think most of the people are dressing "down". Only a few are dressing "up". If people would dress up as they want to, they would be more playful, more colourful. This is the future of everything.

Nobody has to be a diva, they just have to themselves. People have to be free to be themselves. People have enough to be beautiful. I think most of the people are dressing down. A few of them are dressing up. And the idea of dressing up is "up" always dressing up. How you want to dress is your choice. But if people really dressed up like they wanted to, they would be more playful, more colorful. This is the future of everything.

The freedom to allow yourself to be who you are. This might bring a change in the idea of what is called fashion. We are trying too hard to be like others, instead of liking ourselves.

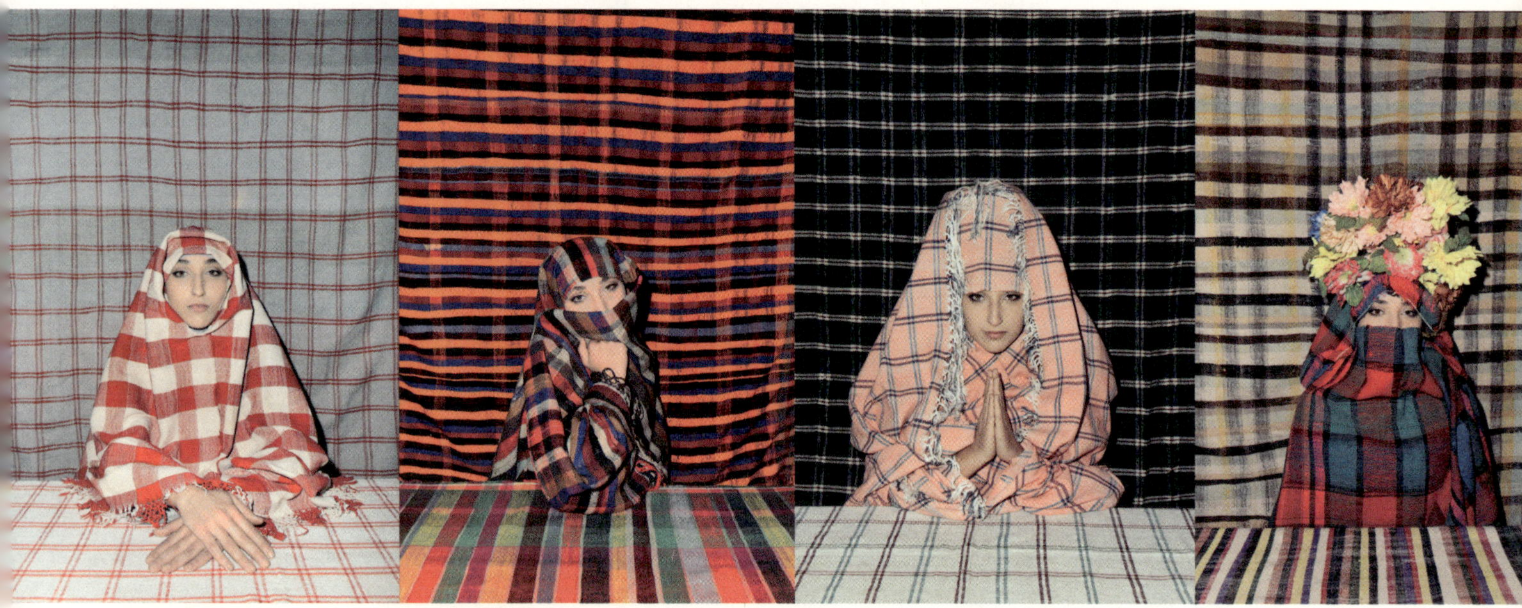

MISS UNDERSTOOD

MISS TAKE

MISS KIDA

MISS ME

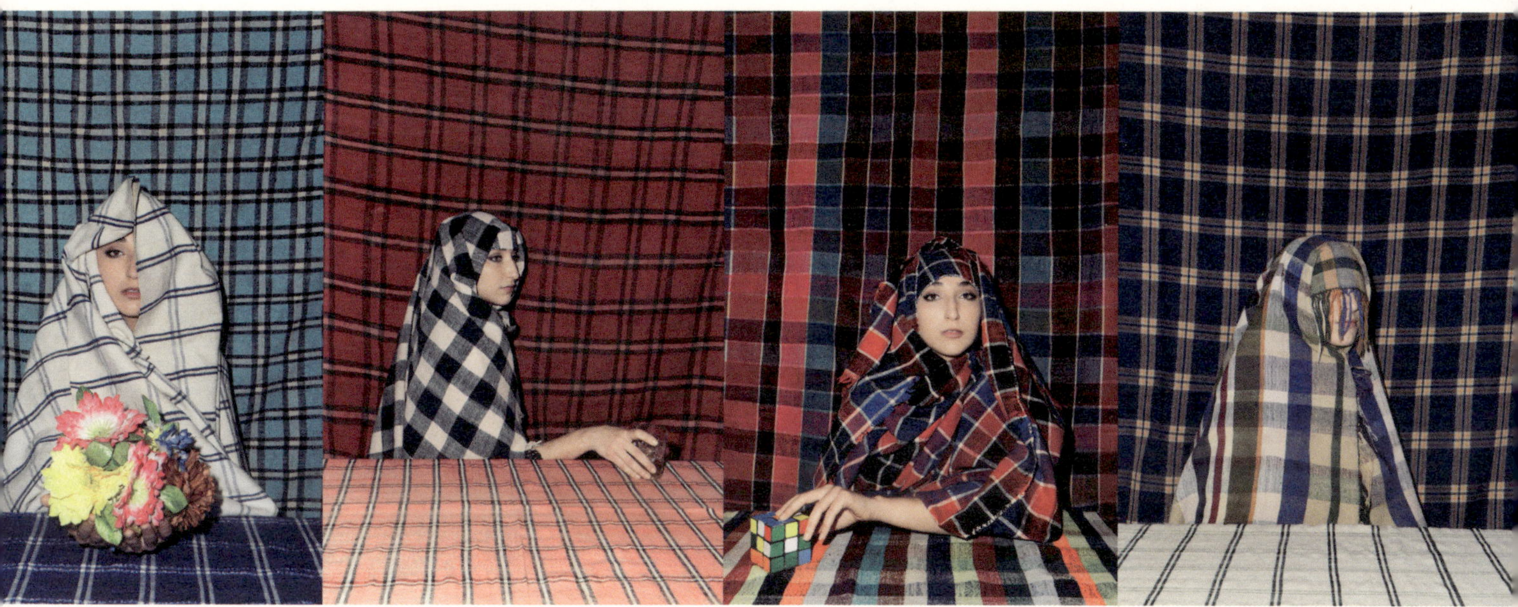

MISS YOU | MISS MAAKOUL | MISS TANNIK | MISS CALL

I thank my beautiful team Bushra, Samira, Paco and my amazing friend, the artist Rinat Aboulafia.
I also would like to thank Sarah Kahloun and Sarah de Scisciolo for making this book possible.

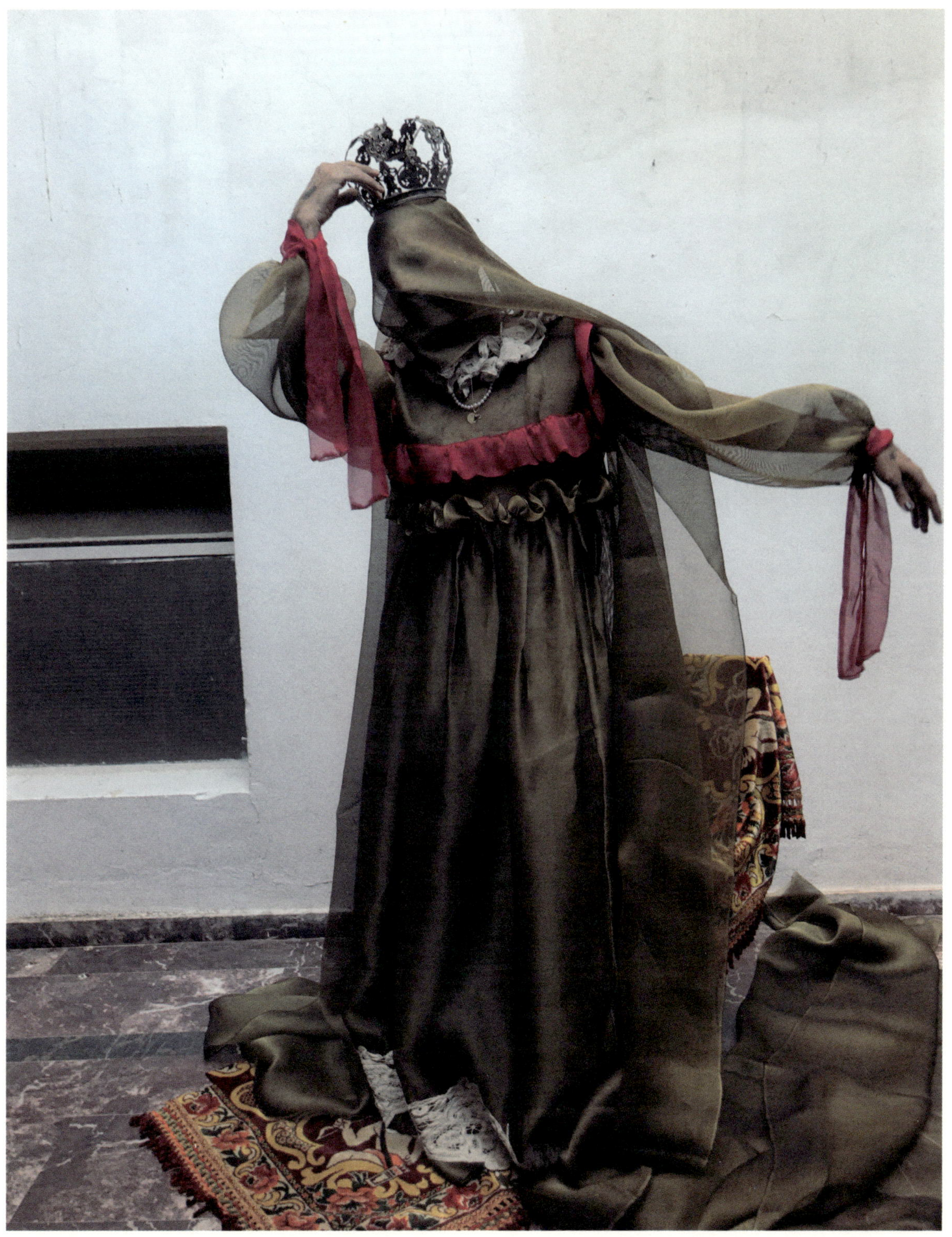

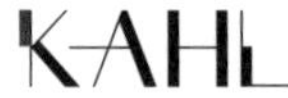

kahleditions.com

Edited & Published by KAHL Editions ltd.
Graphic design KAHL Editions

Printed in October 2017 by KAHL Printing
Printed on Enso Lux Creamy 90g

First edition 2017

ISBN 978-0-9957611-2-4

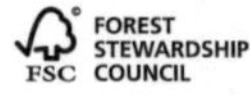

This book was printed according to the internationally accepted FSC standards for environmental management system.

Edition 500 copies

231